WELCOME THEM HOME— HELP THEM HEAL

Pastoral care and ministry with service members returning from war

John Sippola, Chaplain, LTC, ret., MDiv

Amy Blumenshine, MSW, MA

Donald A Tubesing, PhD, MDiv

Valerie Yancey, PhD, RN

Welcome Them Home—Help Them Heal is a "pay-it-forward" pastoral ministry of Elim Lutheran Church of Blackhoof, 2077 County Road 6, Barnum MN 55707. Every $10 you send us will underwrite the publication and distribution of your book PLUS another copy—further extending this ministry of spiritual support to service members returning from war.
Thanks and blessings!

Welcome Them Home—Help Them Heal

John Sippola, Amy Blumenshine, Donald A. Tubesing, and Valerie Yancey

Welcome Them Home—Help Them Heal was produced with a grant from Wheat Ridge Ministries.

The book is also available as an e-book at www.welcomethemhomebook.com.

Edited by: Susan Rubendall
Graphic Artist: Joy Morgan Dey

Printed in the USA

10   9   8   7   6   5   4   3   2

Library of Congress Control Number: 2009925420
ISBN: 978-1-57025-246-4

If you need multiple copies of *Welcome Them Home—Help Them Heal* for your ministry to veterans and their families, contact the publisher:

Whole Person Associates, Inc
210 W Michigan St
Duluth MN 55802

800-247-6789

carlene@wholeperson.com

Dedication & Acknowledgments

This resource book is dedicated to veterans and to their loved ones. They have already sacrificed much and will continue to face the hidden wounds of war long after they return home.

Today we understand better than ever the causes and treatments for many of the medical and mental health conditions afflicting returning veterans. Knowledge alone is not enough. We need to expand the scope of available helping resources for veterans and their families.

The horrors and evils of war experienced by young men and women cause deep wounds to the spirit, conscience, and soul. These wounds often go unrecognized and unattended. Caregivers in communities of faith can make a meaningful difference!

This book was written to equip the growing number of pastors, parish nurses, counselors, and caregivers in churches across the country to support and advocate for veterans and their loved ones. Spiritual recovery after war best takes place in the context of caring, supportive communities of faith that share the news of God's good grace and reconciliation.

We hope this volume will expand your knowledge of how to provide physical, mental, and spiritual care for veterans and spark in you a spirit of willingness and hope.

We have created a website to provide support for caregivers and churches in their work with returning veterans and families. We welcome your emailed questions and comments at **www.welcomethemhomebook.com**. A group of pastoral counselors and therapists who have experience working with veterans is available to help you in your work. Join the conversation. Let us know what your church is doing so that we all can learn from and help each other.

We express our gratitude to those who have given of their time and energy to produce this resource: the group of Vietnam veterans who gathered in Duluth, Minnesota, to share their experiences for the sole purpose of helping recent veterans facing similar challenges; the Iraq/Afghanistan veterans and family members we interviewed and whose stories dot these pages; Kelly Erickson, service member spouse, who helped us create the referral list; and the veterans and members of Elim Lutheran Church of Blackhoof in Barnum, Minnesota who supported this project from the beginning. But, most of all, we offer our heart-felt gratitude to the many veterans who have sacrificed themselves, their families, and their futures in service to their country. Their gifts of courage, persistence, integrity, and service call us to respond in kind.

Special thanks to

Wheat Ridge Ministries

for the Congregational Health and Hope Grant in support of this project.

TABLE OF CONTENTS

INTRODUCTION

Our veterans* are coming home.
We are called to help them heal.

The wars in Iraq and Afghanistan are not yet over, but our veterans are coming home.

Some have completed their military duty.

More will return to Iraq or Afghanistan for another tour.

5,150 have died as of September 2009 and will not return home alive.

35,000 have sustained war injuries, and **20,000** are returning with Purple Hearts.

500,000 carry within them deep, invisible, emotional wounds—unknowable to others, often unknown even to themselves.

Many have lived through life-altering spiritual trauma and will find the quest for peace and reconciliation more difficult than fighting the war.

Too many will commit suicide in the coming years—probably more than the numbers killed in battle.

All—yes ALL—returning service members will experience the challenge of re-entry as they leave the war zone behind and begin to put their lives back together.

When they come home, excitement is in the air! . . . at first.

Anyone who has seen a typical welcome home event understands the public expressions of joy and relief felt by family members. Young children sit on relatives' shoulders to catch a first glimpse of their father or mother. Parents breathe a palpable sigh of relief when they see their son or daughter march onto the tarmac,

Nationwide, more than 96,000 National Guard members and reservists have completed health reassessments since October 2006, and 49 percent reported health problems unrelated to combat wounds.

—U.S. Defense Department Associated Press article in the *Duluth News Tribune*, "Returning Soldiers Come Up Short," Wednesday, November 28, 2007.

In this book we use veterans, service members, and soldiers as generic terms. We refer to specific branches (marines, reservists, etc.) only in relation to specific studies. To reflect the growing prominence of women in the military we have tried to strike a balance on the use of gendered pronouns.

armory, or gym floor. Prayers have been answered, and everyone anticipates that life together can begin once again. Over a few months and with hard work, many veterans and their family members do find a new "normal."

Behind the jubilant homecoming celebrations, however, many returning veterans hide invisible wounds.

Upon returning home, many veterans face the biggest challenge of their lifetime and begin fighting a personal, hidden war in earnest. Often well concealed at first, for many the signs and symptoms of post-war trauma and stress—depression, anxiety, domestic problems, substance abuse, isolation, suicide, and homelessness— eventually appear. According to the U.S. Defense Department, of the 96,000 National Guard members and reservists who have completed health reassessments since October 2006, half have reported health problems unrelated to combat wounds.[1]

"For 33 years we knew something was wrong. But, we didn't really have a clue. And then he finally got help . . . for PTSD. He still has it. But now we understand."

—Mary Jo,
Spouse of a Vietnam veteran

Providing attentive care in the first few months after a veteran returns home is important for several reasons. First, early detection usually results in more effective treatment and better outcomes. Second, early treatment can prevent a cascade of interrelated problems stemming from unaddressed physical, emotional, and spiritual post-war trauma and distress. Loved ones, friends, and close work associates are often the first to notice emerging problems and also become the key people through whom difficulties are initially addressed.

America faces a crisis of care.

Service members and their families face deep spiritual crises not generally in public view. Sufficient resources have not been committed to help returning veterans recover from the traumas of war. To be sure, many good programs are already in place and actively serving returning veterans. Existing governmental programs, however, are stressed to the limit. Adequate numbers of programs, policies, and personnel are not available to meet current needs—and the largest surge of returning veterans has not yet peaked. America, having put forth its best to fight these wars, must now match that effort in helping our sons and daughters heal.

Pastors and churches are called to step forward and respond to this crisis.

Churches are uniquely positioned to help. Many church members have family members and friends who have been personally affected by the conflicts in the Middle East. Although returning veterans are among the demographic least likely to attend church, many have loved ones who attend regularly. With coaching and support, caregivers (pastors, parish nurses, congregation members, loved ones, friends) can be empowered to render an invaluable service to returning veterans. Because the issues are complex, caregivers need education and information to become helpful partners in the readjustment process.

> *Multiple deployments add significant complications to the process of re-adjustment: delayed grief, more difficulty "coming down," and delayed help for PTSD.*

This handbook is intended to help church leaders and members

Identify common post-deployment/re-deployment difficulties

- Discuss the challenges facing returning veterans and their families.

- Recognize common deployment-related symptoms and reactions: post-traumatic stress disorder (PTSD), traumatic brain injury (TBI), depression, combat stress, and moral and spiritual distress.

Develop skills for helping veterans and their families

- Use attentiveness and active listening skills for inviting veterans to tell their stories.

- Learn what to say and what not to say to recently returned veterans.

- Know when and how to make an effective professional referral.

- Walk with veterans in ways that build trust, the most important prerequisite for healing.

- Describe the dynamics of spiritual recovery from war-related trauma.

Make referrals and advocate for soldiers within current military systems

- Become acquainted with the Veterans Administration (VA) benefits and programs.

- Learn how to get contact information for VA, state, and local resources to share with veterans and their family members.

Take positive action steps

- Set up *Circles of Care* within churches.

- Promote a congregational climate for healing.

- Provide assistance to veterans during and after the referral process.

- Use the rich resources within our faith tradition to promote spiritual recovery.

- Join with veterans and their families in our mutually shared, life-long quest for internal peace, reconciliation, and recovery from war-related trauma.

"In a crowd . . . it's been 35 years and I can just now sit around people."

—Larry, Vietnam veteran

KEY POINT

Remember, one size doesn't fit all. Treat soldiers and their families with the same personalized care as you would any family going through a major adjustment or crisis. But now, stir in what you learn here to help you better support and serve soldiers and families.

THANK YOU to those churches that, regardless of members' personal political opinions about this war, have already gone the extra mile to address the needs of the service members and families who carry the burdens and hardships of this difficult conflict. Your prayers and attentive care give comfort to military families and promote a public awareness that helps reduce the isolation many veterans feel.

There is still more we can do! Unfortunately, not long after soldiers are welcomed back home, they are all too often removed from prayer lists and their ongoing needs are forgotten. What people may not know is that most casualties of war occur long after veterans come home. We invite your continued care for veterans throughout their most challenging time—the arduous return to a peaceful life.

Well-informed and skilled church leaders and members can provide an added dimension of care for service members returning to a system woefully lacking in resources and vision. If hundreds of congregations each pay attention to at least one service member and his or her family, we will greatly reduce the casualties in the "war after the war." We invite you to prayerfully consider this call to a long-term ministry of care.

Our veterans have mustered incredible endurance, resourcefulness, teamwork, and bravery to meet the challenges of deployment. As Iraq/Afghanistan troops face the challenges of re-entry, their churches, communities, and country have an opportunity and a responsibility to respond in ways that will positively impact service members, their families, and society. But knowledge is not enough. Churches need leadership, compassion, and commitment to become active partners in the transition process.

Welcome them home and help them heal.

This reference handbook, produced especially for clergy, parish nurses, and church ministry teams, is designed to give you the information and the skills to make a positive difference in the lives of our returning service members and their families for years to come. Study the information thoroughly and keep this reference handy as you partner with veterans and their family members in the healing process. We offer it to you in support of your ministry, as you join with people of faith across the country preparing to welcome them home and help them heal.

JS, AB, DT, VY
May 2009

"The sound of the drums in the contemporary service sometimes drives me batty. They trigger a startle response and I am much more at ease in the traditional service accompanied by piano or organ."

—Fred, WWII veteran
There are many like Fred, who, years later, still suffer from PTSD.

CAREGIVER NOTES

CHAPTER ONE

THE NATURE AND CHALLENGE OF THE IRAQ/ AFGHANISTAN WARS

Understanding the Big Picture

Before detailing the significant challenges our service members face upon returning from war in Iraq and Afghanistan, it is important to consider the big picture. How do we measure or describe these wars?

Do we measure them by their length? If so, the Iraq/Afghanistan Wars have already lasted longer than World War II.

Do we measure them by the $3,000,000,000,000 (3 trillion) dollar total projected price tag? Or do we measure them by the projected 700 billion dollars for post-war health care costs, which amounts to an expenditure of almost $10,000 for every person now living in the U.S.[2]

Do we measure the wars by their casualties? Of the over 1.6 million military personnel who have served, including over 160,000 women, more than 5,150 have died, and over 35,000 have been physically wounded. Of those 1.6 million personnel, roughly one-third will eventually need medical and psychological assistance for war-related problems. These numbers do not include the 100,000 Iraqi citizens (based on the most conservative estimates) who have been killed since 2003, the countless wounded and maimed, and the over 4,000,000 who have left their homes and become refugees.

Do we measure these wars by the emotional and spiritual price veterans and their families will pay during the coming decades? The Vietnam War taught some difficult lessons about the personal and relational price of war. Within six months of return, 38 percent of married Vietnam veterans were divorced. Between 40 and 60 percent of all Vietnam veterans experienced persistent emotional problems. The number of those who died by suicide easily eclipsed the more than 58,000 who died in combat.

THE LONG ROAD HOME

The road home from war is longer, steeper and often more challenging than the road to war for most soldiers and their families. After the joyful, long anticipated reunions there is a difficult period of transition, readjustment, and hard work ahead for every soldier and his or her family. The church can be a helpful partner in the process.

—John Morris,
Beyond the Yellow Ribbon: How churches can help soldiers and their families readjust after combat

Predictions regarding health outcomes for Iraq/Afghanistan War veterans indicate that they will likely fare no better than Vietnam veterans—unless we make changes. A major study by the Rand Center for Military Health Policy Research found that approximately 18.5 percent (300,000) of U.S. service members who have returned from Afghanistan and Iraq currently suffer from PTSD or major depression, and 19.5 percent (320,000) report experiencing a traumatic brain injury. Roughly half of those who need treatment for these conditions seek it, but only slightly more than half who receive treatment get minimally adequate care.[3]

The Uniquely Destructive Character of the Iraq and Afghanistan Wars

All wars can be described in terms of their length, costs, and casualties. The wars in Iraq and Afghanistan, however, pose additional unique challenges to the U.S. military forces and to the health of returning service members. Why is the mental and spiritual trauma of these wars so intense and extensive?

The Coming Home Collaborative, an association of people who are concerned with the psychological and spiritual healing of veterans, responds to this question:

> *"Some features of the Iraq War increase the risk of psychological harm. In most previous wars, the support personnel—the bulk of any army—were behind the lines of combat and removed from immediate danger. In Iraq and Afghanistan, there are no rear lines. There is never a moment to let down one's guard. Service members live bathed in fear for their entire tour; no place feels safe. They know that mortars may hit them in their barracks while they are sleeping, walking about, or while gathered to eat."[4]*

Fighting in an insurgency, where terror tactics are used by the "civilian" enemy, is very complicated. In an insurgency there are no safe zones. Insurgents are difficult to identify. The person you have lunch with in the afternoon may be the person who later tries to kill you. The Green Zone, the supposed haven for diplomats, has been infiltrated by bombers and subjected to regular mortar attacks. The attacks come without warning—a tactic designed to keep combatants on 24-hour alert. Suicide bombers know no boundaries. Many of the service members stationed in Iraq/Afghanistan are at high risk to be killed or wounded for most, if not all, of their deployment.

Furthermore, today's troops serve months without a break. In contrast to World War II, when the goal was to give troops a full month away from combat after serving three months on the front lines, soldiers serving in Iraq and Afghanistan rarely get the breaks experts recommend for emotional survival and recovery. In response to a Congressional task force recommendation, length of tours for Iraq troops was recently (August 2008) decreased from 15 months to the traditional 12 months. Michael Mullen, Chairman of the Joint Chiefs of Staff warns that the reductions will not, however, fully provide the relief needed by overstretched troops and their families.[5] To complicate matters even more, troops serving in Iraq/Aghanistan often return for second, third, and fourth tours of duty, with less than a year at home between tours. Many soldiers being sent back already exhibit symptoms of mental and emotional stress. To begin healing from trauma, a person must first believe that the trauma is over. With frequent re-deployments, that feeling of safety never occurs.

A recent disturbing trend is the growing number of soldiers who are receiving psychotropic (anti-depressants, anti-anxiety agents) medications to help them cope during deployment. Persons using these medications need close monitoring, a standard of medical care unlikely to be available to soldiers in a war zone. The increased use of psychotropic medications for persons in combat leaves many unanswered questions. What impact do these drugs have on unresolved trauma? What happens when a person experiences unrelenting trauma while on medications? Will the use of medications interfere with healing or postpone and complicate long-term recovery?

The Established System of Care for American Veterans

On the battlefield, U.S. soldiers receive the best care in the world. Trauma teams stationed in the field render aid using the latest life-saving techniques. After evacuation, soldiers continue to receive extensive care for combat injuries. Since Vietnam, state-of-the-art medical care has reduced battlefield deaths sevenfold.

Unfortunately, the best battlefield medical care in the world diminishes rapidly both in quantity and quality once the life-and-death crisis is over and the soldiers' physical, mental, and emotional illnesses become long-term. Many are under-diagnosed and once diagnosed, they wait too long to receive treatment. Veterans complain of long waits to receive disability payments.

The Veterans Administration (VA), the government agency tasked to meet the needs of veterans, has not received enough funding to manage the dramatic increase in the need for services. The amount of money allocated by Congress for care does not begin to meet the estimated 700 billion dollars needed for the long-term care of Iraq/Afghanistan War veterans.

The lack of adequate funding and resultant limitation of services is occurring at a time when we know more about the impact of deployment and combat on soldiers' long-term health. Improved diagnostic methods enable health-care professionals to treat more successfully post-traumatic stress disorder (PTSD), traumatic brain injury (TBI) and other serious physical, mental, and emotional war-related conditions. However, large numbers of veterans are not getting care during those critical first months when timely interventions can best prevent unnecessary suffering and worsening of symptoms.

Treatment is clearly most effective when it is received early. Why, then, has our country not allocated the proper resources for those who have risked their futures to serve on our behalf? Why are we willing to pay the costs of engaging in war but not willing to provide the necessary care for those who fought this war for us?

Some suggest that the apparent apathy on the part of the American public regarding veterans' care exists because only a very small percentage of the population is directly affected by the wars. Perhaps the disinterest lies in the perception that the war is being fought by a volunteer army. Maybe the difficulties faced by returning soldiers seem too daunting and too painful for the American public and its leaders to contemplate.

While all of these reasons contribute to the lack of adequate attention and money devoted to the crisis of care experienced by veterans, the most likely reason is that veterans' problems remain largely hidden from public view. Some veterans come home, withdraw, suffer in silence, and try to make sense of their experience in isolation. We romanticize and honor our warriors, cast them as heroes, and then deny the reality of the long-term costs paid by those who have been to war.

Veterans' problems do not go away magically or quickly. Problems

TRAGEDY

A possible outcome of the crisis of care

At 1:30 in the morning in August 2005, a sheriff's helicopter was shot down in the South Valley neighborhood of Albuquerque, New Mexico. The police were chasing a fleeing burglary suspect, and the helicopter was hovering about 100 feet above the housetops with searchlights ablaze when it was hit and downed by ground fire. Miraculously, no one died in the crash.

A Marine veteran and marksman who served in Afghanistan was placed on trial for the shooting. On his return from war, he had become depressed, withdrawn, friendless, and jobless. He was living with his parents, who supported him and tried to get him professional help. He had suffered a spinal cord injury as a result of the war and reportedly suffered from PTSD. Police reports indicate that he had attempted suicide four times.

Undiagnosed and untreated mental health problems in veterans lead to tragic outcomes that impact the veterans, their families, and our communities. This veteran was initially in prison, but later he was released. We wonder what could have been done earlier to avert this tragedy.[6]

ignored, suppressed, and denied will over the years cast an even longer shadow over veterans' lives and futures. When care systems deteriorate, soldiers and their loved ones become casualties of war a second time.

Surfacing Mental Health Problems

As in all major past conflicts, many troops returning from the Middle East have experienced trauma and death at close range. A study published in the New England Journal of Medicine documented that of a particular group of Marines who served six months or more in Iraq, 87 percent knew someone who was injured or killed; 75 percent saw death face-to-face; 57 percent handled human remains; 87 percent shot at the enemy; 65 percent were responsible for a death; 95 percent reported being attacked or ambushed; and 28 percent reported being responsible for the death of a noncombatant.[7]

According to a June 2007 Congressionally-mandated Pentagon study of the problems related to the Iraq conflict, U.S. troops returning from combat in Iraq and Afghanistan suffer daunting and growing psychological problems. Nearly 40 percent of soldiers, 33 percent of Marines and 50 percent of National Guard members report having symptoms of mental health problems. Of the 500,000 troops who have served more than one term, even higher proportions report symptoms of anxiety, depression, and PTSD.[8] Because veterans are reluctant to report, actual rates of symptoms are likely to be higher.

Traumatic brain injury (TBI), the signature injury of this war, compounds other mental health problems. The concussive force delivered by the roadside bombs called improvised explosive devices (IEDs), the weapon of choice used against coalition forces in this conflict, causes brain injuries that increase a soldier's susceptibility to other complications, including PTSD and depression.

As one soldier near Baghdad reported, "IEDs are going off like popcorn." Many troops who have been near an explosion at close range or have experienced multiple explosions suffer some hearing loss and are at high risk for suffering TBI. About 19 percent (320,000) of returning soldiers have received at least one concussion during their tour of duty.[9] Unfortunately, without neurological testing, TBI is virtually indistinguishable from several other mental health problems, thus complicating diagnosis and treatment for this serious condition.

How Do We Currently Respond to the Crisis in Veterans' Care?

Many efforts are underway to respond to the challenges presented by returning veterans. In May 2007, the Senate passed a budget that increased the appropriation for Department of Defense health programs by 3 billion dollars to cover rehabilitation for all amputations and injuries and to provide mental health recovery support. This is an important start, but it is not nearly enough. Our programs, policies, and veteran benefits are outdated—pegged to the costs and cares of World War II, when the majority of these programs were initially implemented.

The VA mental health resources are over-extended at the same time many veterans and families are in dire need of services. To compound the problems, National Guard and Army Reserve soldiers who live in rural areas often lack access to military bases and to cities where services are more available.

Our returning sons and daughters are not dispensable. They are not to be abandoned or betrayed, asked to carry their deep inner pain alone, without care or treatment. Much more is needed. Pastors and congregations are called to step forward and reach out with understanding and love. Churches all over the country, working diligently together on this issue, can make a difference.

The Churches of America Can Respond to this Challenge

Many returning service members are vulnerable to spiritual despair and are asking spiritual questions: What does my life mean anymore? Who can I trust? Why do I feel so depressed? So alone? So hopeless? Why can't I fit in anymore? Where do I belong? How do I live with this recurring terror? How can I manage the emotional pain? The guilt? Who can still love me?

What can church leaders and members do? First, church caregivers must educate themselves on the issues facing veterans and their families. Churches across America have a wealth of resources—pastors, parish nurses, trained visitors, retired social workers and counselors, wise combat veterans, and concerned relatives and church members. Some clergy and lay leaders already have the training and the disposition to offer support to veterans. All congregations, if given basic awareness and some training, can make a significant contribution to their health and well-being. Church leaders can help parishioners identify their unique gifts and callings, inviting them to assist with this mission.

Second, people of faith must believe that they can make a difference! The Church has a primary mission to be on the front lines of offering spiritual support so essential to the full health and healing of returning veterans. Pastors may not realize that the military personnel who give reintegration briefings identify clergy as key resources for service members and loved ones seeking spiritual support after the war. Churches are in an excellent position to provide community-based, faith-centered care and love to people in transition.

Chapter Two describes the challenges that veterans face as they make the transition back into civilian life.

A DEBT WE MUST HONOR

A small percentage of our citizenry—military personnel serving in the Middle East and their families—are making great sacrifices. Many soldiers are returning from the Iraq and Afghanistan wars with combat stress syndrome that has the potential to impair them for life. The civilian helping network— the faith communities especially—need to prepare to help these soldiers and their families heal from spiritual, moral, and psychological wounds. We believe that by intervening appropriately and early, the worst of the consequences suffered after other wars— homelessness, suicide, family homicide—may in many cases be avoided.[11]

—**Coming Home Collaborative**

CAREGIVER NOTES

MAKING THE TRANSITION FROM SOLDIER TO CITIZEN
Understanding Re-entry Challenges

Many veterans report that their transition home was harder than fighting the war. If clergy and church members are going to accompany veterans as they face unique transition challenges, they need to try to understand why a veteran might find the return home so difficult.

Many soldiers come home still carrying their warrior edge inside them—turned on and ready to react in an instant. Every soldier faces the challenge of shedding that warrior persona and adjusting to being a citizen again. This adjustment always takes far more time than the three weeks allotted for post-deployment activities.

Although they have received briefings reminding them how much they and their family members have been changed by the experience of war most soldiers are, nevertheless, unprepared for how difficult their adjustment will be. Soldiers know at some level that they are recovering from combat stress, decompressing from battle fatigue, and transitioning from a unique military environment, but unless they have experienced deployment to a war zone before, they cannot fully comprehend the challenges that lie ahead. At first, most are just happy to have made it home alive.

The Making of a Warrior:
Pre-Deployment, Deployment, and Post-Deployment

There are three major phases in the mobilization of a military unit: pre-deployment, deployment, and post-deployment. While the focus of this book is primarily on post-deployment, a brief description of each phase of the military experience will help us understand the mental, physical, emotional, and spiritual

"I stood at the bus station with my suitcase like an alien in a strange world. Just 24 hours before I was in a bloody firefight where two buddies died just before they were to come home, and now I was home alone and expected to act normal."

—Vietnam veteran

KEY POINT

Pastors, lay leaders, parish nurses, friends, and other people can help best by being aware of the problems and remaining mindful of the soldiers and their loved ones long after they return.

—Nancy Miles
Family Support Coordinator

dynamics of soldiering. Post-deployment challenges are often rooted in pre-deployment training and the harsh realities of deployment activities.

Pre-Deployment: Training for War— The Transition from Civilian to Soldier

From the first day of basic training, a soldier embarks on a strange journey—the road to war. Military training is based on the primary goal of teaching civilians to accomplish military objectives and survive the battle. They are introduced early on to the harsh realities of combat. They learn the best possible procedures to accomplish deadly missions, and they drill until they can clean a weapon in their sleep. They learn to put the welfare of the group ahead of their own safety and trust that their buddies will do the same.

Training exposes soldiers to emotional exhaustion, hunger, sleep deprivation, harsh weather conditions, and the simulation of killing and being killed. From the beginning, training inoculates the conscience, so that a soldier will kill and destroy on command.

Units engage in months of intensive, repetitive training so that in the chaos and fear of a tense situation, they will automatically revert to habit. Survival often depends on the right split-second response. The soldier's mantra is, "Train as you fight so in the crisis you will fight as you've trained."

How do people cope with the sights, sounds and smells of death when they have learned "You shall not kill" throughout their lifetimes? How do they cope with the cries and screams as lives are snuffed out and homes destroyed? Most of us rarely reflect on the fact that the tasks we ask soldiers to do on our behalf are things we would not willingly do ourselves.

While significant training time is dedicated to preparing soldiers to kill, comparatively little time is devoted to helping them cope with the toxic fallout of the actual experience of killing. The real shock and horror of war occurs only as they live through the experience. How do people cope with the sights, sounds, and smells of death when they have learned "You shall not kill" throughout their lifetimes? How do they cope with the memory of hearing the screams of those whose lives are being snuffed out or whose homes are destroyed? Most of us rarely reflect on the fact that the tasks we ask soldiers to do on our behalf are things we would not willingly do ourselves. In normal social contexts, we label many combat behaviors as illegal or sociopathic. We send young men and women into war situations that often push them beyond their human limits.

Deployment: Living through War—
The Transition from Soldier to Warrior

Ramping up for real combat accelerates when soldiers arrive in the theatre of operation. As threats to life become more apparent, soldiers ratchet up to an even higher alert, and the body's survival mechanisms engage. When this happens, the body's chemistry and neurological wiring (referred to as the General Adaptation Syndrome) change as the soldier copes with increased trauma and stress. The soldier's necessarily increased perceptions of threat and fear lead to a "fight or flight" response that begins to operate on hair trigger alert. Without downtime, a soldier remains in a constant state of sympathetic nervous system arousal, experiencing surges of adrenalin for hours and days at a time.

Soldiers must respond skillfully to a set of conflicting roles. A soldier puts on a friendly public front in order to interact positively with potentially hostile citizens and relate to them in a professional manner. Behind the friendly front, however, the soldier is also on ready alert, planning how to kill the persons they encounter should they be enemies in disguise. When in proximity to civilians, soldiers constantly scan for danger.

To be sure, a soldier's life is famous for standing in long lines and putting up with the banalities of military life. Nevertheless, after several months of living in danger, witnessing death at close hand, ducking mortars, and surviving IEDs, most soldiers become hard-wired to respond swiftly and forcefully to any perception of danger. Once that hard-wired response occurs, a soldier has made the internal transition from soldier to warrior. Sometimes the transition happens in the first engagement with the enemy. It may happen with the shedding or drawing of blood. Convinced first hand of the high personal stakes involved in war and made brutally aware of his or her own mortality, the soldier's transition to warrior becomes necessary for survival.

Post-Deployment: Coming Back from War—
The Transition from Warrior to Citizen

The post-deployment phase includes all the work a soldier does when turning towards home, a process called "reintegration." Reintegration involves returning to a world that has changed: family, friends, work, church, community all have moved on, pushed by necessity. For many service members, reintegration also signals the beginning of an internal struggle for survival. Upon return, soldiers must begin to shed the warrior's self-protective alert system and deprogram the physical, mental, and emotional mechanisms and the hyper-vigilance that kept them alive. Shedding the warrior mentality often constitutes the biggest challenge to soldiers in the post-deployment phase.

For most soldiers, it is impossible to suddenly let go of the behaviors that helped them survive the battlefield. It is not possible to flick an off switch for those responses forged under stressful circumstances and reinforced daily. Months and even years of pre-deployment training and desensitization coupled with the actual experience of war become chemically affixed in the brain and require extensive reconditioning to decrease recall and automatic bodily responses.

Some Transitions Go Well

All returning veterans and those close to them will require a transition period when they are reunited. Service members' experiences of reintegration will vary greatly, depending on the types of trauma they experienced and how they internalized those experiences. For many, the transition will go smoothly.

Most soldiers use their three weeks of post-deployment "in-processing" (turning in equipment, paperwork, getting physicals) to decompress from the time they leave combat zones to the time they actually get home. Returning soldiers and family members receive briefings on the challenges they are about to face. Once home, some problems can be prevented, and damage can be minimized when follow-up care is well managed.

Military units that train together, deploy together, fight together, and return together develop strong unit cohesion. A high degree of unit cohesion, coupled with leadership that is perceived as smart and caring, are important variables in maintaining soldier health, well-being, and morale throughout all phases of deployment. Many people know WWII veterans who regularly gather years after their units were disbanded or reconstituted, a testament to the life-sustaining power of unit cohesion.

Building on knowledge regarding the importance of sustaining unit cohesion, some states have instituted programs to provide returning reservists with regular medical and mental health follow-ups in the supportive context of a functioning unit. Soldiers in more cohesive units watch out for and rely on each other after they return home. During the periodic checkups, soldiers are also screened for other deployment-related problems. (See the Minnesota National Guard's program, Beyond the Yellow Ribbon.[12])

Caring leadership and unit-based follow-ups are essential to the health and well-being of returning veterans. Caregivers need to be aware of the types of follow-up care available to service members in their area. They should also know that the quality of care varies depending on the veteran's location. Investigating the types of services available to service members and veterans in your region will help you make the best possible referrals.

Many Transitions Are Difficult

For many soldiers the transition home will be more difficult than they imagined. Too many will never fully make the transition and will struggle for the rest of their lives. Nevertheless, with some good listening and adequate support, the problems faced by most will gradually resolve with the passing of time. Common reintegration challenges include:

Responding rapidly to change. Soldiers spend years in pre-deployment training and in combat activities during their lengthy deployments. In contrast, after two to three short weeks of in-processing, they find themselves suddenly back home, trying to act normal again. The speed of change leads to feelings of culture shock and, at times, psychological immobility.

Adjusting expectations. Service members, along with their family, friends, and work associates, often harbor unrealistic expectations that they will experience a quick, problem-free adjustment to life at home. This is particularly true after a service member's first deployment. Pushed by the necessities of daily life, soldiers try to pick up quickly where they left off. Returning warriors often look deceptively good on the outside, reinforcing the premature expectation that life quickly returns to normal. Recall, however, that warriors are trained to present a positive front, to look good. The veteran has dreamed about coming home. Family members have prayed for this moment. In joyous

> ## KEY POINT
>
> *Unit cohesion is the sense the soldier has of closeness, camaraderie, and caring within the unit. Leadership is the primary influence that holds units together. Effective combat leaders are perceived as caring for both the soldiers and their families. Keeping a good unit together can be extremely helpful, especially during the first critical four to six months after return.*

> *"Three weeks ago I was driving Humvees and kicking down doors, and now after three weeks of demobilization, signing papers, and getting medical checkups, I am suddenly back on the streets at home, but I can't yet make myself understand it or believe it."*
>
> —Iraq veteran

celebration, loved ones finally hug each other again, believing that all is finally well. However, real-life frictions soon arise. Disappointments emerge. Hurt feelings grow. The normal stressors that occur in all relationships become especially difficult for veterans. When expectations for the perfect life after war shatter, veterans and their families commonly ask: "What is wrong with me? With him? With them? With us? Why are we feeling and acting this way? We prayed for this day to come. Why are we fighting so much?"

Making decisions again. During deployment, military commanders make most decisions for soldiers, who must focus on the dangerous job at hand. Soldiers rarely need to ask: What should I eat? Or wear? What should I do this evening? Suddenly back home, returning soldiers face so many choices in their lives that they may feel overwhelmed.

It takes time and a conscious effort for soldiers and their families to relearn how to make trivial and significant life decisions together. On the other hand, soldiers trained to lead others and give orders may have difficulty sharing decision-making with other members of the family.

Adjusting to the slower pace of normal living. In the war zone, service members live on the edge. The adrenalin rush produced by fear and the need to be on constant alert generates excessive bio-chemical stimulation. Life at home without the constant surges of stress hormones may seem boring. Depression may set in. To alleviate boredom and depression, some veterans will engage in higher risk activities like sky-diving, racing, or gambling. Too many will self-medicate with alcohol/drugs or engage in criminal behavior.

Grieving the loss of intimate companionship and close comrades. Not only do many veterans carry the grief of losing friends in battle, upon returning home they also lose the close, meaningful daily relationships with their comrades. Service members live together under threat to their lives twenty-four hours a day. The bonds of immediate intimacy are not easily replicated under normal living conditions—and likely will never be experienced again.

Relating to loved ones again. People hope to connect smoothly and quickly with each other after a period of extended absence.

In reality, everyone has changed dramatically. The process of relearning how to be mutually supportive takes a great deal of time and commitment. Reestablishing a comfortable intimacy with one's partner and with old friends may be difficult at first. When people are separated from each other for many months, they need time to adjust to each other again, even under normal circumstances. For veterans who have experienced war traumas, reestablishing close and intimate relationships will be especially challenging.

Renegotiating the details of living together. While the veteran has been away, the family has attended to all the details of life back home. Upon return, how does the veteran fit back into the details of balancing the checkbook, mowing the grass, doing the shopping, and attending to the kids? All the tasks of living are once again subject to negotiation. Lack of communication skills will inevitably lead to misunderstanding and hurt feelings.

Returning to the old job. When the service member vacated the job, others may have filled in to get the job done. Work patterns have been altered, and it can be tough to fit back into the old job, take pride in old tasks, and enjoy workplace banter and camaraderie.

Dealing with the fatigue of multiple deployments. In the Iraq/Afghanistan wars, many service members have completed two, three, or even four assignments. During the first readjustment, all involved likely functioned at their best and worked very hard to reconnect. Upon return from multiple subsequent deployments, veterans and their families may feel worn out. When readjustment fatigue sets in, people are more likely to say to themselves, "Not this again! We've been through this twice already, and I'm angry and sick and tired of it."

Addressing the challenges of National Guard deployment. For the first time since the Korean war, National Guard troops have been used extensively in the Iraq/Afghanistan wars. The full range of services provided on a military base are often not available to National Guard troops. While rural communities often provide strong support systems from friends, extended families, and community agencies, VA services are usually less available in most rural areas. Many veterans encounter the burden of having to drive several hours to access care. For the same reasons, rural families

"I won't miss Iraq, but I'll miss the people—everyone here is like family."
—Iraq veteran

"I was just happy to see my girlfriend. I thought we would pick up where we left off, get engaged, and marry. Little did I know we would be separated in less than two months."
—Iraq veteran

"For seven months [after my return], I was like a zombie. I was in a haze. I couldn't work. I could hardly function. Finally, I don't know why, I just gradually came out of it."
—Persian Gulf War veteran

"I leaned to shoot to kill a man at 500 yards. I am really good at it. But, there just don't seem to be that many job openings back home for my particular specialty."
—Iraq War marksman

often experience difficulty maintaining connections with military Family Support Groups during long deployments. Therefore, rural veterans, along with their families, often experience an exaggerated sense of disconnect and isolation.

Barriers to Seeking Post-Deployment Help

In a 2004 study of returning troops, only 23 to 40 percent of soldiers who indicated that they suffer from mental health disorders reported that they actually received help.[13] Service members and their families experience powerful and deep-seated barriers to getting help in the post-deployment period—often as a result of military training and attitudes. Understanding the barriers will help us dismantle them so that more veterans and families will both seek and receive the help they need. Service members may be reluctant to seek help for many reasons.

Stigmatization of mental health problems. The military (and society in general) stigmatizes people who have mental health problems. Service members fear disgracing themselves, their command, and their families if they admit to emotional or mental difficulties. Spouses may also be reluctant to report problems that might jeopardize a service member's career.

Lack of resources. In many places, the VA's financial and personnel resources are inadequate to meet the burgeoning demand for care. As the war continues and with multiple and extended tours, the problems will deepen. Too often, getting help is a long and difficult process.

Denial. Trained to override and ignore symptoms of stress-related problems while in a war zone, returning soldiers often deny their problems and try to carry on without help.

Compensation. Service members learn compensation as a survival skill. When interacting with a hostile and potentially deadly public in war zones, soldiers compensate for their internal fear and anxiety by appearing confident and in control on the outside. Veterans take these skills back home and "fake" looking good as a survival mechanism.

Distrust. Military personnel often harbor distrust of both military and non-military counseling professionals. The "counseling types" are considered less than real soldiers. Even talking to the chaplain can be perceived as a sign of weakness.

Expediency. When soldiers return home, they are asked to fill out a form in which, among other things, they are asked about various physical or psychological problems they might be having. Soldiers know that if they admit to having any problems, they might be detained for further evaluation. Many indicate "no problem" simply to get released immediately.

Secrecy. Service members worry that they might be pressured into disclosing secrets. War is horrible. Civilians are killed. People are tortured. Soldiers experience gut wrenching realities first hand, and many soldiers resolve never to talk about what they have seen . . . ever!

According to the Rand Report,[14] service members also identify the following additional barriers:

- The medications that might help have too many side effects—45 percent

- It could harm my career—44 percent

- I could be denied a security clearance—44 percent

- My family or friends would be more helpful than a mental health professional—39 percent

- My coworkers would have less confidence in me if they found out—38 percent

Here are some suggestions for minimizing these barriers so that veterans can more easily and more effectively seek and accept help.

Maintain casual contact and build trust for the long haul—listen and be non-judgmental.

Normalize the process of "getting help." Educate church leaders and members, family, friends, and work associates about barriers, and surround veterans with a culture that says, "It's OK to ask for and receive help when you need it."

Emphasize early identification and preparation in facing the problems of post-deployment. In preparation for combat service members anticipate, identify, and train for the extreme situations they will encounter in war. Remind veterans that they can apply those same problem-solving principles as they face the severe challenges of post-deployment.

"We were involved in a firefight. It was over in minutes. My platoon leader and I carefully walked behind the house. An Iraqi man was huddled in the corner. He was unarmed, afraid, and he raised his hands in a gesture of surrender. The platoon leader pulled out his pistol and shot him three times. 'You never f***ing saw that!' he barked. We walked back around the house. 'What was that all about?' said one of the guys. 'Oh, just a f***ing stray dog,' said the platoon leader."

—Iraq veteran

Play the "courage" card and challenge the veteran to be brave enough to seek treatment. "It takes more courage to face your problems and seek help than to 'suck it up' and go it alone."

Encourage clergy, parish nurses, and caregivers outside the military system to provide a safe and confidential entry point, which may be more acceptable for some veterans.

Listen carefully to the answer when you ask a veteran, "How are things going with adjustments back home?"

Summary

It is understandable that transition to civilian life can be overwhelming. First, soldiers need to unlearn the warrior's survival skills that kept them alive in a war zone. Second, while in a physically depleted and exhausted state, many must deal with all the normal re-entry challenges—high expectations, grief, a rapid pace of change, or taking up a civilian job again. Finally, veterans and families face inbred barriers to getting help and feel safer keeping their real feelings buried deep inside.

It is no wonder the transition is difficult for veterans, and all too often their struggles go unnoticed by others. Casual observers cannot see the internal struggles, emotional turmoil, and psychological barriers experienced by returning service members and their families. One has to pay very close attention to the subtle signals that may emerge.

Those engaged in pastoral care should understand that, for the returning veteran, dismantling the warrior programming takes time and hard work. Churches and religious communities have an opportunity to assist veterans and their families through the complex readjustment process by offering encouragement, empathy, a listening ear, and a caring heart.

Chapter Three describes some of the common conditions and maladies experienced by returning service members.

THE PHYSICAL, PSYCHOLOGICAL, AND SPIRITUAL WOUNDS OF WAR

Understanding the Whole Person Perspective

Deep physical, psychological, and spiritual wounds are the assured outcome of any war. All war-related conditions simultaneously threaten the body, the mind, and the spirit, causing a full range of physical, emotional, mental, and spiritual symptoms. While health problems are usually described as either physical, emotional, or spiritual, we know that, without exception, they all affect the whole person.

> *All war-related conditions simultaneously threaten the body, the mind, and the spirit, causing a full range of physical, emotional, mental, and spiritual symptoms.*

- Is there ever depression without the accompanying physical fatigue and spiritual loss of hope?

- Can one feel deep grief without a corresponding suppressed immune system and internal feelings of survivor guilt?

- Is there ever a brain injury without a lack of ability to concentrate, a sense of foreboding, or a crisis of meaning?

- Does one ever experience intentional and repeated violation of conscience without losing the capacity for intimacy, feeling isolated, or developing stress-related physical symptoms?

This chapter provides you with basic information about nine of the most common physical, psychological, and spiritual conditions that result from war. They are divided into three groups of three. The first group includes Traumatic Brain Injury (TBI), Post-Traumatic Stress Disorder (PTSD), and Depression/Suicide. The second group addresses three military-service related problems: Combat Operational Stress Reaction, Military Sexual Trauma,

*Exposure to toxins during
military service can have
delayed ill effects on a
veteran's physical health
and behavior. As yet,
no one knows whether
there will be an Agent
Orange from the Iraq
and Afghanistan wars.
(See endnote 15, page
110, to learn more about
toxic exposures in war.)
Returning veterans should
write down suspected
exposures and name
witnesses before memory
fades. Stay abreast of
emerging research on the
effects of toxin exposures.*

and Substance Abuse. Finally, this chapter discusses three spiritual maladies often neglected in medical classification systems but commonly experienced by returning soldiers: Soul Wounds, Violated Conscience, and Deep Grief.

As you pay attention to a veteran, you may not observe any of the specific clusters of symptoms outlined for a particular malady. Rather, you might notice a failure to thrive. Medical professionals use this term when a definitive diagnosis cannot be made but something still seems wrong, and the person does not begin to feel better with time. Failure to thrive afflicts many veterans during the first months and years after they return. Pay attention to the appearance of a veteran who is "just not doing well," and ask gently about it as you open the doors of communication and offer encouragement and assistance.

Notice the considerable overlap of symptoms among the conditions described in this chapter and how all of these health issues sound like the same problem. Why is this? While each condition is specific, the toll each takes affects the whole person and often produces the same cluster of symptoms: inability to sleep, confusion, hyper-alertness, depression, isolation, anger, impaired memory, lack of concentration, fatigue, and panic attacks. (See the Wounds of War Assessment in Appendix C.)

Remember, it is not your job to make a definitive clinical diagnosis of any condition. Instead, recognize the symptoms, remain encouraging to the veteran, and make a referral to an appropriate professional when necessary. (See referral sources and screening tools in Appendices A and B.)

We begin by discussing three major conditions, TBI, PTSD, and depression/suicide, commonly experienced by people who have been in combat.

Traumatic Brain Injury (TBI)

TBI is a concussion. Brain tissue is damaged when there is a significant blow to the head and brain tissue slams against the skull. In the current Iraq/Afghanistan war, shock waves from improvised explosive devices (IEDs) or from being thrown around in a vehicle are often the primary cause of TBI. Because IEDs also represent a life-threatening, aggressive assault, the same explosion that damages the brain may also lead to the development of PTSD. Mild damage to the brain can also make a soldier who later experiences additional psychological trauma more vulnerable to PTSD.

Many of the symptoms of TBI are subtle and are easily confused with depression or the general moodiness experienced by combat veterans. Mild concussions also make soldiers vulnerable to depression. Caregivers should be aware of the relationship between mild TBI, PTSD, and depression and should seek help accordingly.

The number of soldiers diagnosed with TBI keeps rising. A recent study suggests that as many as 320,000 troops have suffered some form of TBI. The study also raises the concern that 57 percent of those who reported possible brain injury had not seen a doctor for evaluation.[16] Screenings for concussions are still not routinely done, so ruling out the presence of a concussion is a good starting place if symptoms indicative of TBI are noted.

Physical Symptoms of TBI include:

- chronic headaches;
- dizziness/loss of balance;
- sensory problems, such as blurred or double vision, loss of smell, ringing in the ears, or a bad taste in the mouth;
- memory loss or poor concentration; sluggish thinking;
- loss of executive functions (decision-making, problem-solving);
- feeling unusually tired, chronic fatigue;
- disruption in sleep patterns;
- brief periods of unconsciousness.

Resultant emotional symptoms of TBI often include:

- getting lost or confused;
- having mood changes, irritability, explosive anger, emotional disturbances ;
- emotional shut-down, feeling depressed;
- being easily distracted.

CAREGIVER ALERT

If a returning veteran suffers persistently from depression or stress reactions, consider the possibility of TBI. Ask if he or she ever received a blow to the head, lost consciousness, saw stars, or experienced ringing in the ears during deployment.

Negative coping strategies include:

- self-imposed isolation;
- self-medicating.

Post-Traumatic Stress Disorder (PTSD)

Reports indicate that 300,000 troops have suffered some version of PTSD, and 53 percent of those reporting symptoms have not sought treatment.

PTSD is a common consequence of experiencing extreme trauma. Reports indicate that 300,000 troops have suffered some version of PTSD, and 53 percent of those reporting symptoms have not sought treatment.[17] People in the general population also often develop PTSD after natural disasters, terror episodes, torture, serious accidents, physical deprivation, emotional abuse, or sexual assault. PTSD is characterized by an involuntary re-living of the stressful event, using avoidance and numbing as coping mechanisms, and experiencing arousal symptoms.

Service members routinely and repeatedly experience all of the common causes of PTSD and many more. The Army's first study of the mental health of troops in Iraq found that one in eight soldiers reported PTSD symptoms.[18] With multiple and extended tours of duty those numbers have soared. Now, one in five combat soldiers reports some degree of PTSD, and the numbers who suffer from it are probably even higher.

PTSD—A Brief History

Civil War soldiers experienced problems with anxiety and depression, referred to as soldier's heart, irritable heart, or nostalgia. Many were shot as malingerers. World War I veterans developed shell shock, hysteria, and neurasthenia. Suffering soldiers were sent to the front lines, court-martialed, or shot as shirkers. War neurosis, battle fatigue, and exhaustion were terms used for afflicted World War II combatants. More than 500,000 WWII soldiers were placed in mental hospital beds; thousands received brutal frontal lobotomies (the surgical destruction of the brain lobe controlling emotional responses), and many were drugged into semi-consciousness.[19] No wonder soldiers are often reluctant to talk about their war-related PTSD! It has taken a long time to acknowledge that PTSD, depression, and other anxiety disorders occur as common reactions to extreme or prolonged stress.

PTSD was finally officially recognized as a legitimate condition in 1980, after studying mental health problems in Vietnam veterans. Prior to that, blaming the soldiers seemed the best way to account for why some veterans developed mental health problems and others did not. Some claimed that modern soldiers were not tough enough. Others thought that they lacked the requisite moral or character strength, courage, commitment, determination, or patriotism. There is no evidence whatsoever that personal weakness or character defects predict who might eventually develop PTSD. In the opinion of a veteran who works with homeless veterans, "It's not a matter of *if* you will get PTSD; it's a matter of *when*. If you are exposed to enough trauma, you will most likely experience the disorder."

Characteristics and Symptoms of PTSD

A formal diagnosis of PTSD requires that people report symptoms in each of the following three major symptom categories:

Re-experiencing symptoms. High-powered flashbacks are usually triggered by a sight, sound, or smell that brings back the traumatic event. Common triggers for soldiers are: the sound of a jet or helicopter, a car backfiring, a car accident, slow or busy traffic, a suspicious package on the side of the road, someone carrying a shovel, the smell of spent shells or diesel fuel, seeing a woman wearing a burka, crowds, driving under an overpass, and thunder.

When a soldier has a flashback, he or she returns emotionally and physically to a high stress state. Flashbacks might be experienced as night terrors, nightmares, and lashing out when asleep. During the flashback, the person may relive the fear, helplessness, and horror as if it were happening in the present moment. A person may feel separated from his or her body or have auditory and visual hallucinations. One veteran sitting in a support group experienced a flashback upon hearing the hiss of air coming from a radiator. The sound triggered memories of the death of a buddy who died in his arms from a fatal chest wound. The soldier had blocked out the hissing sound from his memory only to have it triggered by a similar sound years later.

DEFINITION

In post-trauma therapy, "trigger" is a technical term that refers to any sight, sound, smell, etc., that sets off a full-blown reliving of a past traumatic event in the present moment.

CAREGIVER ALERT

Multiple exposures to trauma during deployment and past exposure to trauma during a previous deployment increase the risk of severe, long lasting PTSD. Ask the veteran of multiple deployments to take an inventory of traumatic combat events during each deployment.

Flashback experiences include:

- unwanted thoughts or memories of the traumatic event;
- feeling as if the event is re-occurring in the present moment;
- night terrors or nightmares.

Avoiding and Numbing Symptoms. People avoid stimuli that remind them of the traumatic event: sounds, smells, places, relationships, responsibilities, situations, or people. Some people completely isolate themselves and live like a hermit. Some suppress the most traumatic part of an event or become unable to talk about it. They feel emotionally numb and have difficulty getting in touch with and expressing feelings.

Common avoidance symptoms include:

- isolation;
- self-medication—overuse of drugs and alcohol;
- depression;
- denial;
- emotional shut-down;
- feeling disconnected from one's feelings or other people.

Arousal symptoms. People suffering from PTSD may be in a constant state of alert (hyper-vigilance). Increased emotional arousal can be seen in uncharacteristic outbursts of anger, sleep disturbance, panic, extreme irritability, memory loss, confusion, being easily startled, and having difficulty maintaining focus. High-risk activities sometimes feed a desire for stimulation and a sense of "being alive" that comes with heightened arousal.

Common arousal symptoms include:

- avoidance (avoiding thoughts, activities, places, children, other adults, or conversations associated with the event);
- emotional volatility, violent, angry outbursts, engaging in high risk and high adrenaline activities, easily startled, constant irritability, feeling jumpy, always on alert;
- memory loss, confusion, inability to focus;

- loss of ability to function well in daily life—feeling awkward, unsure, inattentive or over-reactive, difficulty connecting with others (communicating, engaging in sexual activity), inability to concentrate well and assume a full work-load, resulting in poor job performance.

As a result of the dysfunctional patterns that develop over time as veterans attempt to deal with their symptoms of PTSD, they are at increased risk for substance abuse, suicide, separation and divorce, nagging feelings of guilt and shame, low self-esteem, recurring phobias, panic attacks, chronic anxiety, unemployment, and homelessness.

Recovery from PTSD

In the civilian world, of those who experience severe trauma, about 30 percent go on to develop a chronic form of stress disorder that persists throughout their lifetime. The incidence and severity of PTSD symptoms increase when a person has:

- suffered a prior head injury (TBI);

- a history of significant depression, anxiety, or other mental health problems;

- previously learned and adopted poor lifestyle coping mechanisms;

- experienced more intense and long-lasting trauma;

- a very limited personal support system—family, friends, church, and professionals.

Some people recover from PTSD by themselves. However, without support, direction, coaching, or intervention, recovery can be slow, and negative coping methods become even more likely.

Some people recover from PTSD by themselves. However, without support, direction, coaching, or intervention, recovery can be slow and negative coping methods (substance abuse, withdrawal from relationships, use of force) become even more likely. Unfortunately, the angry outbursts, difficulty in keeping appointments, and denial that are characteristic of PTSD sometimes interfere with treatment.

Flashback experiences are a common result of emotional trauma. For many veterans, the flashbacks will diminish with the passing of time. But for others, flashbacks signal the need to seek professional help. Veterans should identify their own personal triggers and inform their loved ones what to expect, so family members are not caught off guard and alarmed by their behavior.

Early intervention and successful stress-management strategies keep psychological and emotional problems from worsening. Veterans need to be reminded and reassured frequently that their symptoms result from the consequences of war and are not their own fault. Over the course of a lifetime, symptoms will come and go, and their intensity may increase or decrease. Many people will never fully recover, but over time, they learn how to manage symptoms so they not only survive—but thrive.

Depression

Many returning veterans experience depression. Depression often has an identifiable cause, such as the death of a buddy, wounds, loss of function, amputation, divorce, trauma, or any stressful situation. Depression typically combines with PTSD, anxiety, TBI, or substance abuse. The type, severity, frequency, and duration of symptoms vary from person to person. Men and women may also experience depression differently. Men tend to focus on physical symptoms, such as loss of sexual desire, agitation, problems sleeping, chronic fatigue. Men more often talk about being angry. Women report feeling hurt, guilty, worthless, and sad.

Symptoms of Depression

Physical symptoms

- fatigue and decreased energy;

- insomnia, early morning wakefulness, or excessive sleeping;

- unusual weight gain or loss; overeating or appetite loss;

- random somatic symptoms—persistent aches, pains, headaches, cramps, or digestive problems that do not respond to treatment.

Emotional/Spiritual symptoms

- persistent sad, anxious, or empty feelings;

- ongoing moods of hopelessness or pessimism;

- heavy sense of guilt, worthlessness, or helplessness;

- loss of interest in activities or hobbies once pleasurable, including sex;

- excessive anger or restlessness;
- thoughts of suicide or suicide attempts.

A veteran's depressed state may be compounded by a tendency to isolate themselves from others and to self-medicate. The returning warrior experiences alienation because of the unique experiences (both good and bad) of war. Feelings of isolation can breed hopelessness and may be prompted by:

- the inability or resistance to talk about war experiences with those who haven't been there.

- the belief that friends and co-workers have leapt ahead in life—gone on to school, married, received promotions, learned new skills, and advanced in their careers—leaving the soldier behind, frozen in time.

- the overwhelming but impossible need to catch up quickly.

- feeling uncomfortable in crowds. Large groups of people, in worship for example, may generate fear, anxiety, and panic.

Suicide

Suicide is always a risk for anyone who suffers from clinical depression or PTSD. Veterans are at higher risk, especially those who report feeling immersed in death during their wartime service. The suicide rate for military veterans is twice as high as that of the general public, and it's an astonishing four times higher for the current group of veterans in the 18–24 age range.[20] Furthermore, because of stigma, shame, religious concerns, and insurance issues, suicide deaths are under-reported—often ruled as accidental. Although it is impossible to report accurate numbers, some data suggest that three times as many Vietnam veterans have killed themselves after returning home as were killed in the war.[21] The current trend of post-deployment suicides may put veterans returning from Iraq/Afghanistan on a similar lamentable path.

Veterans are at particularly high risk for suicide for several reasons. Familiarity with and access to weapons provides them with available lethal means. The danger of suicide increases significantly with the addition of substance abuse, particularly

CAREGIVER ALERT

ALWAYS take a depressed veteran's threat of suicide seriously. Don't be afraid to ask if he or she has a plan. Ask directly, "Have you had thoughts about hurting yourself before?" "Do you have a plan to end your life?" Asking will not trigger a suicide attempt! A thought-out plan usually indicates higher risk, as does the break-up of a relationship, especially for males. In the case of a suicide threat, it may be necessary to escort the person to a professional caregiver or facility or stay with him or her until help arrives and a care plan is established. If the person poses a danger to himself or herself, emergency care, assessment, treatment, and even hospitalization may be necessary. Before the soldier returns home, ask if the treatment plan includes safely locking up pills and weapons and a follow-up plan.

with the depressive effects of alcohol. The brutalities of war create hopelessness and despair. Soldiers have become familiar with death. One female veteran of the first Gulf War remembers coming home thinking there was no reason for people not to kill themselves if they wanted to.

Warning signs of suicide

- talking or writing about dying, death, or suicide;
- hopelessness, rage, and uncontrolled anger;
- making good-bye gestures (giving away possessions, buying gifts, calling military buddies for closure);
- expressing despair at having no reason to live;
- feeling trapped and obsessing about death (e.g. frequently visiting graves).

Warning signs unique to veterans

- wearing parts of a military uniform;
- obsessive preoccupation with war (e.g. constantly viewing military TV channels);
- obsessive preoccupation with weapons (e.g. carrying, sleeping with, cleaning one's weapon).

We continue by discussing three additional problems related to military service: Combat Operational Stress Reaction, Military Sexual Trauma, and Substance Abuse.

Combat Operational Stress Reaction (COSR)

Combat operational stress reaction (COSR) is a military term for the short-term response to the direct experience of traumatic events. Combat stress reactions manifest themselves as extreme fear, anxiety, fatigue, and internal pressure—normal feelings experienced by soldiers in hostile environments. Imagine living with the 24/7 awareness that any moment you might be obliterated in a blast while in your bed or at dinner. Most soldiers who have been in or around combat zones experience combat stress. Special units treat and debrief soldiers soon after a traumatic event to minimize the psychological damage. However, in fast-paced operations, the quality of the debriefings varies, and most units must improvise on their own. Soldiers who have experienced any of the following circumstances likely have experienced some degree of combat stress:

- have been fired upon or have killed others;
- survived a blast (or multiple blasts) from an IED;
- witnessed the severe wounding or death of a buddy;
- experienced the smell or stench of dead bodies;
- handled the dead; witnessed or tried to rescue someone who was dying;
- witnessed or handled people with severe burns;
- lived in constant danger of injury or death;
- worried about nuclear, biological, or chemical attack;
- survived an accident— sometimes in hostile circumstances;
- lived in extremely harsh, de-humanizing conditions, exposed to the elements, often carrying extra pounds of equipment and layers of body armor;
- suffered dehydration or heat stroke;
- experienced overwork, sleep deprivation, fatigue, and exhaustion;
- maintained 24/7 hyper-alertness in all of the above conditions.

Actions considered to be war crimes are particularly troublesome to soldiers:

- mercy killings;
- atrocities or torture of soldiers, civilians, or animals;
- indiscriminate killing of non-combatants.

Common reactions to combat stress include:

- fatigue and trouble sleeping;
- nightmares and night sweats;
- uncontrollable shaking and dizziness;
- emotional bursts of anger, fear, anxiety;

KEY POINT

Combat operational stress reaction may not meet the diagnostic criteria that qualify a veteran for financial assistance. Nevertheless, COSR can be extremely debilitating and negatively affect all aspects of life, including one's relationships and the ability to hold a job.

- violent outbursts (e.g. throwing, hitting, kicking);
- nausea; loss of bowel or bladder control;
- trouble focusing, remembering, or making decisions.

The military claims that for the majority of soldiers these reactions pass relatively quickly and do not develop into more serious long-term problems. We are unaware of any longitudinal studies that corroborate this claim, and while that might be good news, combat operational stress reactions can also become more complex and chronic if not given proper attention.

Military Sexual Trauma (MST)

Military sexual trauma is usually perpetrated by another service member. Over 160,000 women have served in the current conflict. Nearly one third of female veterans who seek help at VA facilities report having been a victim of rape or attempted rape while serving in the military.[22]

The stress for a female service member multiplies. While fighting for her country, she also has to guard against assault from her comrades. Fear of sexual assault and harassment pose serious problems for both women and men. Being sexually assaulted by someone who is supposed to be supporting and protecting you—especially someone higher in the chain of command—is particularly egregious. Because of the military's poor record of prosecuting and convicting offenders, many victims choose to endure rather than report.

There is a growing awareness of military rapes perpetrated by males against males. Men who have been assaulted are at higher risk for substance abuse and suicide.[23] Because of the shame and stigma associated with male rape, assaults are rarely reported.

The aftershock symptoms of sexual trauma often manifest themselves in PTSD. Sexual trauma can also impact the veteran and his or her intimate relationships in the following ways:

- low self-esteem, making it difficult to experience personal intimacy;
- inability to perform sexually and enjoy sexual contact;
- overly aggressive sexual behavior;

"When my platoon sergeant sexually assaulted me while I was sleeping I immediately told my commander. He told me to talk to the chaplain who listened but didn't do anything about it. For many years I buried it with booze. This has plagued me and caused serious intimacy problems in my marriage of over 15 years."

—Male Gulf War veteran

- preoccupation with sexual activity;

- distorted sense of intimacy vs. physical sexual activity;

- low energy due to lethargy, depression, and chronic fatigue;

- inability to experience pleasure;

- inability to "lose control" during sexual activity;

- personal inhibition as a result of PTSD.

It is important for pastors and parish nurses to be aware of the potential for sexual trauma during military service. While it may be difficult to initiate the conversation, it is important to ask service members if they experienced or witnessed sexual harassment, unwanted touching, or sexual assault.

CAREGIVER ALERT

Because of boundary concerns we recommend that women talk with women about sexual matters. Note that some men may more easily disclose sexual trauma to a woman.

Substance Abuse

Some deployed service members may not have had access to drugs or alcohol, so when they return home they start making up for lost time. Others may have had ready access to drugs and have grown to rely on them to cope with the stressors of war.

Why is the use of alcohol and other drugs such a common post-combat problem? In the immediate moment, mood-altering substances work. They take the edge off the symptoms and the emotional pain. However, many soldiers move beyond social use to problem use. They become reliant on this dysfunctional pattern of coping, and the negative effects begin to impact the soldier's entire life—a DUI, a hangover that diminishes job performance, an angry late night fight with one's spouse. When the use of consciousness-numbing drugs becomes an uncontrolled habit, it turns into an addiction.

Addictive symptoms include the compulsive need to use a substance regularly, maintaining secrecy, and denial about the extent of use, and a pattern of blacking out. Veterans who become addicted need substance-abuse treatment as well as treatment for other underlying problems.

By the time they reach help, veterans may already be suffering from several conditions layered one on top of the other—the original TBI or panic attacks and the resultant addiction to problem-creating coping behaviors. For example, a veteran suffering from undiagnosed PTSD may become depressed. To cope with the depression, he self-medicates with alcohol or drugs and develops a substance-abuse problem. The veteran eventually gets a DUI and enters treatment for chemical dependency. A good therapist is always on the alert for the underlying causes of behavioral problems so that both the substance addiction and its exacerbating conditions can be treated successfully.

Spiritual Maladies

In the Christian tradition, war has long been regarded as a gross consequence of human failure. The conduct of war too often descends into brutality. And even when war brings a semblance of peace, the road is littered with the dead and bereaved and with broken, shattered lives and relationships. A sense of brokenness and alienation from God, self, and others is one of the predictable consequences of war.

When it becomes acceptable to hurt or kill neighbors and destroy their homes and livelihoods, war becomes a blatant source of evil. War normalizes the abnormal and puts service members and civilians in circumstances where they are constantly forced to evaluate and choose between killing and being killed.

Most descriptions of the health problems experienced by veterans give only a passing nod to spiritual maladies. This omission is unfortunate because some of the causes of trauma have spiritual roots. For example, the experience of killing others and living with the threat of being killed is especially traumatic because prohibitions against such actions are deeply rooted in one's sense of self and obligations to others.

While some soldiers emerge from war spiritually intact and grow even stronger, many more return with a deep sense of brokenness and despair. Bruised, battered, and violated spirits easily succumb to nihilism, the sense that nothing matters anymore. Ask a soldier in such a condition if his "give a shit" is broken, and he will know immediately what you are talking about. The loss of hope and meaning gives evidence of a deep spiritual wound—one that cannot be healed by medication alone.

In the following section we identify three spiritual maladies that

> *. . . the experience of killing others and living with the threat of being killed is especially traumatic because prohibitions against such actions are rooted deep in one's sense of self and obligations to others.*

are all too common consequences of war: Soul Wounds, Violated Conscience, and Deep Grief.

Soul Wounds

"Soul" is the nexus of our deep connection with all that is good, true, and beautiful: our connection with the rest of creation and our connection to God, whose essential nature is divine love and in whose image we are created. Soul wounds result in a diminishment of everything meaningful to the person. They erode the human capacity for connection, trust, gratitude, appreciation, creativity, playfulness, compassion, forgiveness, peace, hope, love, and zest for life itself.

It is not a coincidence that many veterans use religious language to describe the ravages of war. "The war stole my soul." "I died spiritually." "I saw evil firsthand—the monster in myself and in others." The words "soul," "spiritual death," and "evil" communicate an overwhelming personal experience of sin, concrete experiences of evil, and a profound separation from God, self, and others.

Countless veterans describe the dark side of their war experiences with another word—hell. "War is hell." "I lived through hell." "I experienced my own personal hell." Soul wounds, sober manifestations of an invisible spiritual malady, feel like hell at the very core of the soldier's being. Many veterans put the lid on their hell and suffer a hellish existence alone, living with a silence that further deteriorates their relationships with God, self, and others.

The Violated Conscience

Spiritual well-being and the health of the soul are intimately related to ethics and morality. Any intentional perpetration of harm towards human beings, their livelihood, and their belongings can cause grave moral injury and damage the relationship to one's self, others, and God. War unleashes massive, destructive internal and external forces that wound the soul and usher in moral failure.

Our moral life is intimately related to the spiritual sentinel called the conscience. In war, the moral first yields to the amoral. The amoral then easily leads to acts of immorality. When a person acts in immoral ways, the conscience is breached. The resulting guilt and shame festers—often to erupt years later.

> "Everything spiritual that had formed the foundations of my soul and guidance in life felt like a lie, as did my social teachings. My soul had been scooped and cleaned out just as one scrapes a pumpkin to make a jack-o'-lantern. Every seed, every strand of pulp of my beliefs were gone. I was souled out, and the windows to my soul . . . [the thousand-yard stare apparent in the eyes] were positive proof."
>
> —Michael Orban
> *Souled Out: A Memoir of War and Inner Peace*[24]

War regularly puts human beings in impossible moral dilemmas. Killing a person to protect one's buddies can violate a sensitive conscience. Being ordered or goaded into participating in the mistreatment of prisoners or civilians is, for some, a forced violation of personal values that can lead to an abyss of spiritual despair.

We hear and appreciate the many stories of bravery and of missions that bring hard-won peace to war-ravaged communities. There is, however, a dark and vicious side to war that most of the public does not hear and see. The destruction wrought by bombs on human beings, homes, and work places is brutal beyond comprehension. Insurgency tactics can be particularly depraved and dehumanizing. Insurgent fighters justify the use of terror tactics (e.g. suicide bombing, torture, killing of civilians, slitting of throats) as necessary strategies to win against a well-equipped occupation force that can wreak havoc from a distance. Occupying forces too often retaliate with similar brutal tactics in the belief that they need to fight fire with fire.

While the horrors of war may not be the rule, neither are they rare exceptions.

While the horrors of war may not be the rule, neither are they rare exceptions. Fearful of ambushes, supply convoys run over innocent civilians. In coping with that horror, soldiers use black humor and joke about "road kill." Buildings get targeted and destroyed even though it's not known whether people are inside. Homes are commandeered and families driven out just because the bivouacking soldiers want to locate where there is better satellite television reception. Innocent people are arrested to fill "suspect quotas." Soldiers terrorize and humiliate men in front of their wives and children. Raids leave homes in shambles. Faced with making quick judgments, checkpoint guards sometimes kill unarmed, harmless people. The stakes are extremely high when one is charged with protecting one's comrades.

Group attitudes and norms reinforce inhumane behavior. Encouraged to overcome their reluctance to hurt others and their aversion to gore, soldiers will sometimes mutilate and desecrate corpses. Most of these actions carry a taboo against public disclosure. Unfortunately, keeping the secret can give such offenses more power over the soldier, further wounding an already violated conscience.

We have seen graphic portrayals and heard stories of torture at the hands of our own soldiers. Congressional hearings and independent studies have documented both incidences of torture and command decisions to torture. What happens to soldiers who are ordered to participate in torture? News media reported that one soldier, Alysson Peterson, after refusing to use torture for interrogation, committed suicide. Group norms plus command approval make it almost impossible for a soldier to refuse to follow an order.

One does not have to be a direct participant in violent acts to experience the wounding of soul and conscience. Being a witness to killing, torture, and destruction of property can cause severe moral injury. Many veterans are deeply disturbed about killing civilians, especially women and children, but often feel compelled to do so for their own safety.

The physical problems and mental health conditions caused by war are only the tip of the iceberg. At the deepest level of one's being, war cuts people off from their core moral values, forces them to violate their most deeply held standards, and often leaves them feeling lost, unworthy, and alone. We are all called to share the moral burdens, responsibilities, and grief of service members and their families, remembering that anything they have done is the direct consequence of our having sent them to war.

Sometimes people think, "I would never do those things!" If you believe that such behavior is beyond you, you are mistaken. One can never predict how one will respond under the incredibly intense pressures of war. War can bring out the worst in anyone, even in those we consider the most moral and upstanding.

Deep Grief

Everyone experiences grief after a significant loss. Grief can be defined as the experiences (feelings, thoughts, intentions, sensations, actions) resulting from a specific loss or cluster of losses. In war soldiers experience multiple losses. Losses may be mild (e.g. missing anniversaries, graduations, not being home to care for a sick spouse) or more severe (e.g. death of a buddy or a loved one back home, failure of an intimate relationship, loss of limbs, bodily functions, or mental capacities) or spiritual (e.g. loss of confidence, the capacity to love, or a sense of hope or faith in God).

Common immediate responses to sudden loss include shock, disbelief, feeling disconnected, a sense of being powerless, and numbness. As the initial shock and numbness subside, a person will often experience other reactions such as difficulty sleeping, nightmares, difficulty focusing and concentrating, physical exhaustion, loss of appetite, emotional release, or intense experiences of:

- anger or sadness;

- guilt and shame;

- loss of emotional control—tears, groaning, howling, sobbing;

- mental confusion and trouble getting back to normal;

- feelings of hopelessness, joylessness, and despair.

Because survival needs come first, soldiers in a war zone often put their grief on hold. The grief surfaces when they return home, sometimes months or years later. Soldiers are often surprised and confused by the intensity and immediacy of suppressed grief— feeling as if the loss just happened. The close relationship between trauma, depression, and multiple losses creates a tangled web. It takes time and hard work to unravel the tangles by identifying the losses and the feelings associated with each one.

In working with grief, encourage service members to utilize lament as a way to express the full force of feelings such as sadness, hatred, abject despair, loneliness, lostness, confusion, terror, and rage. A lamentation is essentially a personal poem about pain and grief. Lament gives voice to the heart's wrenching and the soul's pain. It is Jesus' cry of abandonment, "My God, my God, why have you forsaken me;" King David's hoarse mumbling grief, "Absalom, my son, my son . . . ;" the depressed Paul's "sighs too deep for words;" and the church's, "Lord, have mercy." Lament is being totally honest with God. As veterans throughout the ages have struggled with the most difficult aspects of their grief, they have discovered that expressing their grief through lament provides a way through the pain and a path to healing.

The Church's Mission of Re-integration, Restoration, and Reconciliation

Walking with veterans and their families on healing journeys is part of the Church's ministry. We recognize that Christ died a torturous death precisely because of our broken relationship with God and each other, symbolized graphically in the images of war and its desolation. "He descended into hell," a phrase regularly confessed by Christians, reminds us of the Good News that even the "hell" of war is not beyond the grasp of God's redeeming love. After the resurrection, the Crucified Victim returned, not with vengeance, but with forgiveness, healing, hope, and a commission to go and do likewise. This is Good News! Chapter 4 offers vision, help, and hope for the healing of returning service members.

Chapters Four to Six will explore how caregivers can better serve returning service members and their families in the context of a community of faith.

CAREGIVER NOTES

CHAPTER FOUR

THE CHURCH'S ROLE #1

Basic Principles for Reaching Out

N o two veterans have the same war experience, nor, upon returning from war do they face exactly the same reintegration challenges. Likewise, veterans heal and recover in their own ways and along their own timelines. Caregivers who understand the healing power of story can offer hope. Pastors who understand the dynamics of forgiveness and reconciliation, spiritual direction, and confessional dialogue can greatly assist veterans in their quest for peace and reconciliation. Parish nurses who gain an understanding of the health issues facing returning veterans can provide preliminary health care screenings, locate treatment resources, and advocate for veterans and their families when they receive substandard medical care. Working together, compassionate, knowledgeable, and skilled caregivers, friends, and professionals can give veterans life-saving and life-giving care and support.

The diagnosis and medical treatment for TBI, PTSD, and depression fall primarily within the purview of a physician or a qualified therapist. However, all caring people have the ability to play a supportive role in helping veterans and their families to heal. Here are some basic principles for walking with soldiers and their families on their healing journeys.

Basic Principle #1
Listen and Encourage Self-Expression

For many returning veterans, the most difficult part of the journey is finding the road to internal peace and reconciliation. Careful, attentive listening to a soldier's story can be a life-giving and, in some cases, a life-saving action.

> ## CAREGIVER ALERT
>
> *A soldier is taking a huge leap of faith when he or she begins to tell you a story. So, always listen—even if you're unsure. If you show obvious discomfort, the soldier will usually read your non-verbal cues and stop talking. If you hang in there, giving verbal and non-verbal indications that you are really serious about paying attention, you encourage the person to go on speaking.*

The Healing Power of Story

Telling even a small snippet of one's story and feeling heard and accepted may be the first important step toward healing. These first tellings may be accompanied by heavy discharge of feelings or by emotional numbness. But, as the veteran tells and retells the unvarnished story in different settings to trusted people, he or she slowly comes to grips with and begins to accept and integrate what happened.

Attentive, nonjudgmental listening will help the veteran in his or her spiritual struggle to sort things out and gain valuable perspective.

Veterans may conceal difficult aspects of their stories. They may experience horrendous memories, flashbacks, and night terrors in connection with what they went through. Stories of trauma are often laden with pronounced guilt and shame.

When told for the first time or to someone new, the story often comes out jumbled and disjointed. The sequence may not be clear to the teller or the listener. If that happens, just keep listening. The teller may need to stumble around a bit before he or she finds the story line, or figures out what should be said. The fear of losing control and unleashing long suppressed feelings in the telling of a story can be terrifying. This is normal. A good listener waits patiently through these struggles. Be prepared for the following dynamics in listening to veterans' stories.

- A soldier will sometimes make politically incorrect comments to see if you react. If you react negatively to an off-hand comment or off-color joke, the soldier may conclude that you do not have the capacity to bear the full brunt of the traumatic experience.

- Sometimes, in an attempt to make a connection, people say something like, "I understand how you feel." A veteran rightly believes that unless you have been in combat yourself, you can't ever fully understand. Don't claim what is not yours.

- Often when telling a war story, a soldier may string together a litany of four-letter words. Don't interrupt or correct the speaker's choice of language. Your job is to listen.

"I locked it away inside, but now I know that more people understand what happens to vets, and that has helped me to talk about it. After three years . . . now I don't think there's anything I wouldn't say."

—Iraq veteran

"It's been 35 years and I just started talking about this two years ago. There are still some things I can't talk about."

—Vietnam veteran

"When I was with my buddy, we could talk about what happened. We could get angry and laugh about a lot of things. But we avoided the parts where we felt sad and shameful. We avoided the grief. When I started looking at the grief in therapy, when I started to cry over what had happened, that's when I finally started putting it all together."

—Vietnam veteran

- For obvious reasons, veterans may appear surly and angry. Develop a thick skin so you can stay in an active listening mode. The veteran's anger is not about you, so don't take it personally.

- Don't change the subject! Doing so sends the signal, "I'm really not interested. I really don't want to hear your story—or that part of your story."

Above all, maintain a calm, compassionate presence. When a veteran trusts you, he or she may tell you something about current destructive behaviors such as getting drunk, driving recklessly, slapping a family member, or having emotional outbursts. If you recoil in discomfort and judgment, the veteran's trust in you will vanish.

Assess the level of danger the veteran is to self and others. If the self-destructive behavior is high risk and has become a pattern (three or more times) make a referral to a therapist or counselor. If a person is already in therapy, ask if he or she has told the therapist about the problem, and be sure to keep listening. If the behavior under discussion has happened only once or twice, this can be an important "teachable moment." Gain helpful information by asking:

- "Did you notice what led up to _____? What were the warning signs?"

- "What did you learn?"

- "What will you do differently . . . next time?"

Basic Principle #2
Relate to the Veteran, Not the War

Avoid interjecting your own politics into conversations with veterans. People ask returning veterans, "How can you fight in this war when you know we shouldn't be there?" Others greet soldiers with an overenthusiastic welcome. "Hey, great to have you back home! What was it like kicking ass over there?"

As public opinion shifts away from military involvement in war, negative feelings about war are all too easily projected on the returning veterans (Vietnam effect). Veterans and their families have had first-hand experiences with the ravages of war.

"When I returned I wondered if I would be able to be honest and tell my loved ones what really happened to me. I experienced some really bad things in the war. When I returned home, they had a nice welcome party for me. Later that evening, I was with three of my close friends. We were sitting in the TV room, and my best friend said, 'We're really glad you're back, and we're really interested in hearing everything that happened to you.' I was relieved, and I started to tell them about some of the missions we carried out. My heart was pounding as I was going to tell them more of what really happened. My friend interrupted, 'Hey, can you tell us about that later? Lost is on at 8 o'clock, and we don't want to miss it.' I was like . . . in shock. No one ever asked about my story again. And I decided never to talk about it ever again. So, I buried it."

—Iraq veteran

Many have had friends or acquaintances killed or wounded. They resent what they perceive as judgments targeted at them, their fellow veterans, and their service—by people who have not "been there." Whether one is for or against a war, the political arena is the proper place to address those concerns not with the returning service member. Be aware how your beliefs and attitudes toward the war might show disrespect, undermine trust, and jeopardize your relationship with veterans and their loved ones. Sensitivity, tact, and discernment are crucial as you build a helpful relationship with the veteran.

There are times, however, when it is appropriate to speak about the larger issues of war. In the prophetic role, a preacher is called upon to speak truth to power. Most veterans respect and value the courage of a knowledgeable preacher who takes a hard public stand against political decisions that unnecessarily put service members' lives and futures at risk.

Basic Principle #3
Offer Honest Encouragement

Offer veterans the following assurances, based on the wisdom of others who have healed after returning from war.

- **It's not your fault.** Your struggles, whatever form they take, **are not your fault** nor are they signs of weakness. You do not need to feel guilty, ashamed, or afraid about them. The painful or fearful reactions you are having to what happened to you are normal and natural. There is nothing wrong with you for feeling as you do. Do not judge your own progress by comparing it to others' responses. Everyone reacts differently to stress and trauma. Accept your own experiences and reactions as your own. Your feelings are alerting you to where you need healing and help. You may feel crazy, but you are not crazy.

- **You are capable.** You learned what it took to survive in combat. Use those same abilities and gifts to develop a new set of life skills. Use your intelligence, determination, capacity for hard work and willingness to learn what it took to be a good soldier to rebuild your life after military service. You are capable and you

Use your intelligence, determination, capacity for hard work and willingness to learn what it took to be a good soldier to rebuild your life after military service.

can adapt. You can and will get better even though you might not believe it at the moment.

- **Accept your experience.** As much as you want to ignore your feelings and deny them, healing begins when you are able to come to grips with your current reality. Even if your situation feels hopeless at this time, you cannot move forward without the truth. Suppressing or denying feelings as a coping mechanism helped you stay alive in a hostile combat environment. In fact, denying some feelings and realities for a while can serve as an effective protective mechanism even after the combat is over.

- **Listen to your feelings.** Staying in denial, however, does not help you heal over the long haul. When you are ready, let your feelings trickle back into your consciousness. Facing the reality of your situation will help you recapture your power over confusing, frightening feelings. You don't need to wallow in your feelings, but you will need to acknowledge and deal with them for healing to occur.

- **Face your fear.** Certain feelings (e.g. panic, depression, despair, anxiety, guilt, and grief) will return from time to time. This may raise your anxiety level—"Oh, no, not that again!" These emotions will most likely surface at an inconvenient time. Of course, there is never a convenient time to re-experience difficult feelings. If you know in advance that some fear and anxiety always accompany the acknowledgement of difficult feelings and experiences, you can more easily keep your anxiety in check.

- **Give yourself permission to falter.** You may panic and think, "I am getting worse again." That's likely not the case. You will develop strategies for dealing with the undesired flashbacks and memories and learn to move on with confidence. Know your warning signs and build strategies to avoid them or predict and prepare for them. Over time, the difficult thoughts and feelings will come to you less frequently, but realize that they could pop back into your life at any time. That, too, is normal. Give yourself permission to falter and don't believe that having a rough stretch means you are failing in your recovery process. The ups and downs are virtually guaranteed.

- **You will improve.** Despite the fact that you may fear that you will always feel the way you do right now, THINGS WILL CHANGE. Your experiences and traumas will always be a part of you. Despite the fact that at the moment it may be hard for you to feel hope for the future, hang on. Many have been where you are now and have improved enough to live a rich and full life.

Basic Principle #4
Encourage Self-Care

The ultimate goal for any returning veteran is to learn to survive and succeed in a post-war environment. Basic requirements include patience, practicing new routines, adopting life-giving activities, and establishing a new "normal" that will lead to a more promising way of life. Unfortunately, when people feel afraid, depressed, or threatened, they often care for their bodies poorly. Under stress or in crisis conditions, we ignore common-sense coping behaviors. If a person already drinks coffee or alcohol, when stressed he or she drinks even more. People worried about their problems sleep less, even though they are exhausted. If eating high-sugar, high-fat foods gives comfort, a stressed person eats even more. Crisis situations tend to undo a person's regular schedule. Preoccupation with worry derails exercise routines.

A well-established trail of medical research has documented the connection between physical health and chronic stress. Being subjected to stressful circumstances over long periods of time can have negative effects on the heart, immune function, digestion, and nervous system. The stress hormones adrenalin and cortisol directly communicate with the cells of each body system through the chemical substrates of emotions.[25] Although it is beyond the scope of this book to discuss physiological medical conditions in detail, veterans should be alerted to the need for periodic checkups and follow-up for diagnosed medical conditions. Many conditions, such as high blood pressure and digestive disorders, can be effectively managed with medications. Stress-related medical conditions also respond well to positive lifestyle practices. Encourage veterans, loved ones, and caregivers to develop positive self-care habits.

Establish a support system. Veterans and their families are notorious for going it alone. The transition home becomes easier when veterans have a group of solid friends they can call upon at any time. Invite veterans to describe how they typically respond in a crisis and ask them to share that information with close friends so their friends won't get overly alarmed or confused when they hit bottom. Ask veterans if they know others who have been through similar experiences and if they can share their stories with them. Suggest that veterans consider choosing people who are not in their immediate families, as those closest to them may need a break from the stress as well.

Practice centering and meditation. Relax. Slow down. Take it easy. Breathe. Be gentle with yourself. Pray. Meditate. Take a long relaxing bath. Enjoy nature.

Adopt a wellness lifestyle. Restful sleep, good nutrition, and regular exercise help rebuild the biological foundation for recovery. Get some exercise every day. Regular exercise has been shown to minimize depression and create a sense of well-being. Eat well. Minimize drinking of alcohol. Get a good night's rest and take naps. Take your meds. Find ways to get a good laugh.

Basic Principle #5
Refer and Support

Caregivers can best help returning veterans by making appropriate referrals and providing support throughout and beyond the referral. Whenever possible, help them find a veterans' support group. Meeting with a group of veterans helps remove the powerful stigma of war-related trauma. Veterans speak the same language, share similar experiences, know the same geographical areas, and understand the craziness of war. Together, they can all realize that they aren't the only ones who have had debilitating experiences. In this "wounded band of brothers and sisters," veterans find hope and healing from isolation, guilt, and shame. They learn how to manage flashbacks and night terrors. They begin to understand that character flaws, moral deficiency, or lack of courage did not cause their problems. With the compassion born of a shared experience, many veterans maintain contact with each other long after the formal therapy sessions end.

Veterans frequently need help learning how to cope with their anger. They have been exposed to many situations that evoked in them intense anger and have learned to use anger, a natural emotion, as a way to respond to any perceived threats to their safety or well-being. It is not the anger itself that is the problem, but rather ineffective or inappropriate management of this powerful feeling. Learning how to acknowledge and appropriately express one's anger is often done in the setting of professionally run anger management classes. Making referrals for assistance with anger management may help veterans differentiate between "legitimate" anger and pent-up hostility and will help them bind the wounds that sustain prolonged periods of anger and rage.

Many veterans and/or family members would benefit from individual or family therapy. Find therapists in your area who are skilled in working with veterans and refer when appropriate.

After making a referral, support the veteran through and beyond the formal therapy process. Continue to hold the veteran and their loved ones in prayer. Check in periodically while he or she is in therapy. When checking in, ask how things are going and be prepared to listen attentively. If the veteran has shared key insights gained from therapy with you, reinforce the importance of what has been learned. You cannot fix many of the consequences of war-related stress, but sometimes a simple phone call or affirmation makes a world of difference to a struggling veteran.

A network of caring people is a vital asset to recovery. Veterans and spouses often talk about key people who helped them along the way, each person filling an important role. Recall that veterans tend to isolate themselves from others. If a veteran who regularly attended church before deployment is absent after deployment, reach out to that person with acceptance and welcome. Good support usually comes in small, consistent doses over the long haul. And the cumulative sum of that support can help minimize the problems for returning veterans and their families.

Basic Principle #6
Pray

At every opportunity, offer public and private prayers with and for returning service members and their families. One pastoral caregiver lights a prayer candle symbolizing the light of Christ and, in her daily meditation, regularly brings all those in her care, including service members and families, to that light. The spiritual discipline of prayer:

- helps maintain a creative spiritual connection, awareness, and focus.

- encourages a healthy detachment from one's concerns as God's mysterious presence and spiritual support is affirmed.

- brings immediate support and comfort to families in stress.

Basic Principle #7
Be Genuine and Trustworthy

Veterans returning from war have been in an environment where they reflexively learned to distrust and view all civilians as potential enemies. Now they must undertake the major spiritual task of learning to interact with people and shift to a higher level of trust. This is not an easy task for those who have learned to survive by being wary of everyone. Veterans may feel strangely vulnerable and distrustful at worship and other church gatherings, not sure if they are safe and secure. Learning to trust people in the congregation can be an important step in reintegration. Only when church members are viewed by veterans as people who are trustworthy and safe can they make the transition from distrust to trust, from vulnerability to safety.

Trusted people in the church provide a therapeutic bridge to civilian life. To build trust, be sure you maintain confidentiality, keep your appointments, and follow through on your promises. If you say you will check in on the spouse once a month, do it. Be consistent. It is better not to make a promise than to make one you can't keep. Veterans' "BS detectors" are finely tuned. They can instantly sense when a person is not being genuine. Above all, be honest in your interactions.

Basic Principle #8
Care for the Caregivers

Caregivers and close family members experience "compassion fatigue" or "vicarious trauma." There may come a time when you, as a caregiver, feel you don't have any energy or desire left. You may begin to hope that people don't raise difficult questions.

Maybe the veteran you once liked has become the person you now avoid. When a person in your care suffers a major setback, you may feel guilty and worry that you might have done something wrong. Your sleep may become disturbed. You might feel psychically numb. You might begin to believe that most situations are hopeless and can't be improved.

Close family members may begin to resent all the care and attention given to the veteran. You may feel alone and begin to imagine that other people just do not care or want to understand the heavy burdens you carry. Your feelings are understandable and common. Even seasoned therapists with good support and boundaries commonly experience compassion fatigue.

How can caregivers and family members stay healthy?

The tips offered here apply to veterans, family members, and caregivers alike. When you start to feel depleted, sit down and read this chapter over once again, but this time read it with yourself in mind. Acknowledge your limitations. Some people are better suited than others for the intense work of dealing with survivors of traumatic events. Taking a break from exposure to stressful situations can help you return more refreshed and effective when you pick up your work again. Remember, you are only human. You are worth being cared for, too!

The basic principles discussed here apply to everyone, not just veterans. None of these eight principles are easy to sustain. However, neither are they all that complex or anxiety producing. Your love and concern for veterans and their family members will show through if you demonstrate sincere interest in them and appreciation for their uniqueness. Part of caring for yourself is to hold those intentions in your heart, take a deep breath, relax, and look forward to making meaningful connections with the veterans and families in your midst.

Chapter Five outlines a series of concepts and practices to help churches and caregivers create and maintain an environment conducive to healing, health, and wholeness.

CAREGIVER NOTES

THE CHURCH'S ROLE #2
Create a Healing Environment

Creating a safe environment conducive to healing is the primary task of churches choosing to work with veterans and their families. Many pastors and congregations may have a long history with the family, having walked with them through crises and important life milestones. Skilled caregivers and parish nurses may also have a history with veterans and their loved ones. Rural congregations often enjoy strong intergenerational ties and extended circles of friends and relatives who can provide long-term support.

Returning veterans and their families quickly calibrate the safety of any setting and decide if people can or cannot be trusted. Here are some ideas that will build trust with veterans and help churches maintain a climate for healing.

"We lived some distance from our immediate family, and it was our pastor and the people outside our family who understood what was happening and breathed life into us."

—Karen, spouse of Iraq veteran killed in action

#1 Be Tactful

Be tactful when talking with veterans and relate to the person, not to the war. Take a personal inventory of your own attitudes and beliefs about the war. This will help you get in touch with your blind spots and remind you of the harm veterans experience when people project their views about the war on the service members themselves.

Members of congregations committed to ministry with veterans should prayerfully contemplate the experience of veterans returning from war. The stakes are high and the costs of the war are very personal. The veteran may have seen comrades wounded, killed, and maimed. Many feel resentful that much of the American public seems more interested in a pop star's foibles than in the life and death struggles going on in Afghanistan and Iraq. They are returning to communities in which many people believe that the country was intentionally misled into war, that it has been conducted poorly, or that the costs far outweigh the benefits.

Remember, veterans want their service, the deaths of fellow soldiers, and the sacrifices of their families to count for something important. They, too, may feel conflicted about the war. Many service members will be sorting out their own thinking about the war for years to come. In the meantime, they need a safe place.

#2 Offer Hospitality

Offering hospitality is a primary mission of most congregations. Behind the scenes in most hospitable churches are capable church staff, flexible custodians, courteous hosts and leaders who know how to extend a warm and gracious welcome.

Churches can offer the use of their buildings as a simple way to extend hospitality to veterans' groups in need of a place to meet. Veterans' groups usually provide facilitators for their own meetings, but churches with access to reputable professionals might also make those resources available. Veterans' support groups provide vital lifelines to returning soldiers. They offer the experience of a hard won empathy and an intuitive sense of timing that is helpful to other veterans. In addition to offering space in the building, ask how the church might be of further assistance.

Spouses, significant others, and parents also need help as they work through the transitional period. A church might offer space and hospitality for spouse/family groups or plan informational sessions to which other community members are invited. Providing childcare at the church during meetings greatly facilitates the maintenance of a successful spouse group. Once a veterans' or family support group takes hold, the word usually spreads and others are drawn to the group.

#3 Hold Veterans and Families in Prayer

Many churches have prayer chains, prayer partners, or individuals who pray for special needs during the week. Other churches regularly include veterans and families in the Sunday morning prayers during worship. Don't drop service members and families from the prayer list after the homecoming. Remember, this will be the most challenging time for some! Intentional, structured prayer for veterans and families in transition and for those who accompany them lies at the heart of the Church's mission and serves as leavening to create a climate of hope and healing.

#4 Create a Circle of Care

A circle of care is a small group within the church that is committed to providing care for veterans and their loved ones. Veterans, especially those suffering the invisible wounds of war, often benefit from a small group of trusted people who offer a nucleus of safety within the larger congregational structure.

Invite veterans and their families to consider being part of a circle of care. Ask them to select two or three people they trust to be in their care circle. To keep contacts manageable, have them designate one person as a primary contact who checks in with them at mutually agreed upon intervals. When a parish nurse is available, we recommend that the nurse be an advisor to the care circle.

#5 Remember Veterans and Families in Weekly Staff Meetings

Even small churches with part-time staff can schedule weekly staff meetings and prayer time. In your planning and prayers, include returning veterans and their loved ones and others who are going through transitions and crises. Regular pastoral practices and disciplines that keep the needs of others at the center of ministry help create and sustain a consistent climate of care within the congregation.

#6 Take the Military Context of the Service Member into Consideration

Each phase of active military service poses a unique context and challenge for service members and their families. Churches pledging to walk with people throughout their military service need a long-term strategy that begins when service members are first notified that they will be "walking through the valley of the shadow of death." The sooner pastoral connections with service members and families are made, the stronger the bond and foundation of trust will be throughout the entire experience. Pastoral care and counsel is also very important for service members who want to maintain their moral values during deployment. Here are some practical suggestions for how caregivers might connect with service members and families through all phases of military service.

Phase I: Pre-Deployment

The anxiety of service members and loved ones understandably escalates when the military unit to which they are attached receives notice of deployment. Notification of deployment sets in motion the psychological, spiritual, and social adjustments needed to prepare for war.

During pre-deployment, service members complete family care plans, which include making provisions for the care of children, drawing up wills, designating powers of attorney, securing health insurance, and arranging for access to finances. Here are some suggestions for supporting service members and families who face imminent separation.

- Shortly after the unit receives notice for deployment, call on the soldier and family and offer prayer, care, and support.

- Ask soldiers and family members what they need from their church, pastor, or parish nurse during this time.

- Maintain regular contact with the soldier and family as they prepare for separation.

- Pray for soldiers and families in the anxiety-laden weeks before deployment.

- Conduct a sending ritual for the soldier and family before he or she leaves. Ask whether they prefer this be done privately or as part of the worship service.

- Be intentional about saying a personal good-bye to a soldier leaving for war.

- Check in with family members within a few days after the soldier has left home.

- Follow through on promises and commitments.

Pre-deployment counseling: Pastors have a unique role as *caretakers of the soul*. Service members and families preparing for war expect that the service member will be in physical peril. Some understand that war also poses perils to the soul. In pre-deployment counseling, remind the men and women going to war of Whose they are. Assure them that their faith community will hold them in prayer, support their loved ones while they are deployed, and help them re-adjust when they return.

Give soon-to-be warriors opportunity to raise spiritual and moral concerns. Ask them if they have thought about how they might act in challenging circumstances. They are probably way ahead of you and will appreciate your willingness to talk about it openly. When people have talked about a moral dilemma before it happens and have rehearsed how they should behave in those circumstances, they are more likely to act in a manner consistent with their values.

Disclosure of torture and abuse, reports of civilians being shot at checkpoints and convoys running over non-combatants raise concerns for those facing deployment. Many fear that they, too, will come under extreme pressure to do things they believe are wrong. Service members need to know that pastors are willing to agonize with them in their spiritual struggles as they prepare for deployment.

Some men and women about to go to war may ask about conscientious objection and their church's stand on the war. Be familiar with the stand your church or denomination has taken (if any) and the rationale for that stand. Some denominations stand against all war in principle, and most members obtain conscientious objector status. Mainline churches consider war a gross consequence of human sin and yet view some war as a necessary evil. Most mainline churches still employ some version of "just war" criteria as a guideline for assessing the morality and ethics of war. The overly simplified version is summarized by the three "Cs,"—cause, conduct, and consequence. Just war criteria considers: 1) the cause for going to war (only as a last resort after all reasonable and sustained efforts have been exhausted and only in defense); 2) how the war is conducted (no intentional killing of noncombatants); and 3) the consequences of the war (the benefits must exceed the costs). For a war to be considered just, all three criteria must be met.

"Before I left for war, my father told me to try to stick by my values. In the confusion of one battle, we overran enemy positions. I suddenly came upon an enemy soldier who stood up and raised his hands in surrender from his foxhole. The captain of our company ordered me to shoot him. I refused and quickly walked away fearing that he might shoot me for disobeying his order. I turned around just in time to see him walk up and shoot the soldier. I credit my father's counsel for my action in that situation."

—WWII veteran

Phase II: Deployment

Many people have witnessed the tearful, lingering good-byes of married service members in the nation's airports. The stress and grief of separation is intense for those staying at home. Churches provide support and maintain relationships with service members and loved ones throughout deployment in the following ways.

- Reach out to the family members left behind. No longer able to fulfill family roles as they normally would, service members receive great peace of mind knowing that their loved ones have people on whom they can lean. Don't forget significant others: the fiancé, girlfriend, boyfriend, or close friends.

- Regularly include service members and families in the prayers of the church. Prayer reminds us of their on-going need for love and care.

- Communicate directly with service members. They thrive on messages from home—letters, emails, picture postcards, care packages, and videotapes. When the pastor sends an email, or especially a handwritten note, it can be like fresh water in the desert.

- Display pictures of deployed service members in the fellowship hall or the church narthex.

- Send church bulletins or newsletters to deployed service members.

- Church groups—Sunday School, Men's, Women's, Youth Groups, Befriender, or Stephen Ministers—can take turns sending care packages or notes.

- Offer to help spouses with child care. Some families welcome a surrogate grandparent to help kids get to activities to which their missing mother or father would have accompanied them.

- Provide space in the church for families to meet during the week.

- Provide practical support: shoveling snow, mowing the lawn, household projects, auto repair.

- Consider providing child care for service members' families. Note: when a congregation provides child care, it has both a moral and legal obligation to review the qualifications and background of the care providers. When the service member's family asks a church member for babysitting assistance, obviously they are making that decision themselves.

- Pay particular attention to the day-to-day needs of families with infants and small children. Single parents can become overwhelmed by multiple concerns. In church and in the nursery, surround children with caring adults for reassurance and affirmation.

- Sunday school teachers, youth workers, and ministers can provide much-needed support for children, pre-teens and youth. For example, one youth worker asked a teen to show her father's location in Iraq on the map and talk about her experiences.

Phase III: Post-Deployment

Treat service members and their loved ones with the same personalized care as you would any family going through a major transitional crisis. Church members can accompany service members and their families as they transition back from war in the following ways.

- Attend the unit's official "welcome home" civic ceremonies. The service member will appreciate the effort you made to be there.

- Welcome the service member personally, "We're really glad you're home!"

- Schedule your church's usual hospitality welcome ritual either at worship (during announcements or prayers) or fellowship time (with an announcement and food).

- Acknowledge the service member's return in the church bulletin and in the newsletter.

- At church, greet the service member with a handshake and a warm, "Welcome home."

CAREGIVER ALERT

Before scheduling welcome celebrations, ceremonies, or rituals, get permission from the service member and family. Many returning service members feel overwhelmed by large groups of people and may not like having attention showered on them. Get their permission and discuss their preferences before making plans.

- Prayers upon return might include:

  > appreciation for the sacrifices and risks taken with the intent of bettering the world;

  > gratitude for their safe return and reunion with loved ones;

  > remembrances of those wounded in body, mind, or spirit, and those who were killed;

  > requests for God's care and guidance during the transition period.

- With the permission of the service member and family, continue to name them in public prayer throughout their transition.

- Initiate communication by phone or a brief visit within the first couple of weeks.

- If you know the service member well, invite him or her out for lunch or coffee after they have been home for a while.

- Reassure service members and their loved ones of the congregation's willingness to help as needed and let service members know with whom they might talk regarding any concerns.

- Offer or help arrange child care so a couple can spend quiet time together early after the return.

- Consider offering to sponsor a couple at a marriage retreat designed to help service members and their spouses deal with post-deployment transition issues.

- Inquire at appropriate intervals about the service member's transition process: "How is it going for you?" "How are things going at work?" "Can I be of help?"

- In a private setting, ask if the service member is experiencing difficulties being in church. One veteran, for example, did not like the contemporary service because of the drum sounds that reminded him of gunfire.

- Tell the service member that, when they are ready, the church will be eager to utilize their skills and gifts for the mission of the church.

- Do not engage veterans in casual conversation about the justness of the war. For them, such conversations about the war will never be casual.

Re-Deployment

Many service members experience multiple deployments that tax them beyond their limits. Be aware of the higher incidences of PTSD, depression, and the concomitant risks of suicide that attend multiple deployments. Because of the higher risks involved with multiple deployments, caring for soldiers and loved ones between deployments is even more critical. Here are some suggestions for ministry between deployments:

- Be alert for undiagnosed or under-diagnosed PTSD and depression in soldiers facing re-deployment. For example, a general screening from a parish nurse may surface the need for further assessment before a soldier is ready for re-deployment.

- Watch for delayed PTSD or delayed grief.

#8 Join Together in the Quest for Peace and Reconciliation

Having experienced grievous wounds to their souls, many returning veterans embark on a long spiritual quest for forgiveness, peace, and reconciliation. The church is no stranger to such quests. Saint Paul struggled mightily as he made the transition from persecutor to apostle. Like Paul, the rest of Jesus' followers, many of whom felt that they were also complicit in his death, negotiated the difficult path to peace only after the disturbing encounters with Jesus, the victim, in the resurrection narratives. Those encounters were both reconciling and transforming.

For many years, pastors have played a key role in helping veterans find peace of heart and mind. Problems rooted in spiritual ground respond to the fruits of the spirit: hope, love, patience, forgiveness, trust, and comfort. Rest assured that the message of the Gospel, communicated through your words and pastoral presence, carry remarkable healing power. If you model hope and forgiveness in your actions and have confidence in the Gospel's healing power, your faith will be evident to the struggling veterans as you walk with them through very dark times.

> **KEY POINT**
>
> *Non-judgmental listening provides space for bruised souls to begin to heal and lays the foundation for reconciliation. The mere non-judgmental reception of the story alone can be powerful affirmation of acceptance and forgiveness.*

"Killing people, that's one of the big issues. Your conscience is telling you, you ain't supposed to be doing this! But you have to. You don't even think about it . . . until later. Do you ever get forgiven for some of the stuff you do?"

—Combat veteran

Confession and Forgiveness

Forgiveness from war-related trauma may be very complicated and elusive. Some veterans do not like the person they have become and get mired in shame and self-loathing. Some carry deep rage and anger at others, thinking they will never be able to forgive. Many soldiers do not realize their need for forgiveness until years later. Others compartmentalize what happened, suffer in silence, and take their experiences with the accompanying guilt and shame to their graves. At some point many veterans wonder, "Can I be forgiven for what happened, for what I did?" "Can I forgive others for violations against me?" "Can I forgive myself?" Lamentably, many veterans never find forgiveness and end their lives prematurely with acts of self-destruction. For some veterans, however, the time comes when they seek forgiveness and reconciliation.

Listeners Need to Prepare for Confessional Conversation

Veterans seeking forgiveness and reconciliation after war-related trauma bear heavy burdens and embark on a strenuous journey of self-reflection. The people to whom soldiers make their confession share in this difficult (but liberating) process. As you prepare for your role as listener, consider what you will bring to the conversation.

For most veterans the road to reconciliation often begins with the telling and retelling of the more difficult parts of their story. When a veteran delves into confessional material for the first time, listeners need to be prepared for disturbing accounts and intense emotional release. You need to first ask yourself, "Am I prepared? Am I ready to hear, accept, and forgive?" You may be distressed at your own honest admissions.

Be alert to subtle shifts in tone and content that indicate the move to confessional mode. Veterans signal the need and desire for forgiveness differently. Perhaps you notice that a veteran seems to be withholding a key part of the story. This can mean a person is up against a stumbling block or getting closer to disclosing a secret. When this happens, indicate your willingness to listen. Be direct and invite further conversation, "It seems that you're up against something really hard to talk about. Do you want to try and get it out?" Sometimes the move to darker dialogue is the culmination of a long relational dance in which the veteran moves back and forth in conversations with you. Perhaps the veteran has been testing the waters of the relationship waiting for the right time to take the plunge and would welcome an invitation.

There are two kinds of confessional conversation. In the more common informal confessional conversations, the confessional elements are imbedded in the story itself. Less commonly, veterans will ask for a formal rite of reconciliation for which some preparation is needed. Traditional rites of confession and forgiveness have been practiced within the church for centuries and provide a safe, life-giving, and affirming formal structure especially to those who have a history of participation in religious rituals.

Whether informal or formal, the presence of another human being during confessional conversation is important for many reasons.

- Another human being can offer immediate support, coaching, comfort, or challenge.

- There is power in the pronouncement that comes through the living voice of another human being who can identify and empathize with the wrongdoer's frailties and can also empathize with those who were wronged.

- The presence of another human being interacting face to face with the veteran can help externalize the guilt often associated with traumatic events and can make forgiveness more concrete.

- Confession may help slow down or even stop obsessive recycling of a disturbing event.

If a veteran repeatedly seeks forgiveness for the same issue, he or she may benefit from professional help for an unresolved psychological or spiritual issue.

Finally, take care of yourself. Use your best self-care strategies for calming your own bodily reactions during and after emotionally charged, intimate conversations.

The Veteran Needs to Prepare

Preparation for confession, forgiveness, and reconciliation assumes some capacity on the part of the veteran to discern wrong-doing

Guilt and shame are easily confused. Guilt relates to one's actions or inactions, about what one did or did not do. Shame is experienced as a severe diminishing of one's sense of self, extreme embarrassment that "I" did or did not do something, or a deep humiliation for what was done to me. The shame-filled person feels that he or she is a bad person, unworthy of others' admiration or care. The antidote to **guilt** is compassionate understanding and forgiveness of the transgression. The antidote to **shame** is compassionate understanding and acceptance of the person.

The veteran suffering from PTSD and depression will always be at higher risk for suicide. Pushing for or inviting disclosure before a veteran has learned to manage his or her PTSD or depression can heighten the risk of suicide. Always err on the side of safety and address suicide risk first.

_____

If veterans are reluctant to share their stories, ashamed of potential emotional release, encourage them to write their stories. Writing can help veterans work through raw, intense emotions and grief—and help them gain the perspective needed to come to grips with moral responsibility for violations committed or sustained.

(violations sustained as well as violations committed), assess appropriate responsibility (excluding false guilt and survivor guilt), and the willingness to make amends.

For some, preparation happens quickly. Some veterans have a clear understanding of their wartime experiences, know what they need to talk about, and understand what they need to do. Others may not recognize even obvious damage done to themselves and others. Most fall somewhere in between. Haunted by horrendous memories, preparation can take a long time—even years. Some may need guidance from a pastor, counselor, or another veteran to discern specific wrongs and assess appropriate responsibility. Most confessional conversations occur over time in a longer process of sorting things out in a way that gradually brings about clarity.

> *"For years I felt guilty over the death of a buddy in a firefight. It was ten years later, after I talked with his widow and heard her say, 'It's OK,' that I finally began to let go of the guilt and move on."*
>
> —Vietnam veteran

Reconciliation is a process. While there may come a precise moment when a veteran wants to talk about key material, reconciliation most often happens in the truthful telling and retelling of the story over a longer period of time. Sometimes the story needs to be told to a specific person the veteran identifies as an agent of acceptance and forgiveness.

The Alcoholic Anonymous fourth step practice of "taking a searching and fearless moral inventory" can be instructive at this point. The process of taking inventory invites people to consider seriously their relationships with God, self, and others while asking themselves "What experiences helped or harmed this relationship, and what role did I play in what happened?" Veterans must come to grips with the most grievous circumstances in which people were killed or in which they experienced direct threats to their own lives at the hands of others. The most difficult incidents for veterans to recall are those acts considered to be war crimes: the killing of innocent civilians, torture, atrocities, sexual assault—any actions that might have legal consequences. It takes courage to face these things, and those who do it need support and encouragement throughout the process.

Coming to grips with guilt. One of the most difficult challenges in confessional conversation is to make a sober and appropriate assignment of guilt. Many veterans have a skewed perception of guilt. They tend to operate within a small, personalized framework, and many unreflectively accept full responsibility for their actions because they signed up or took the oath. Many veterans feel responsible for traumatic events over which they had no control, or they take on all of the guilt in situations of shared responsibility.

Veterans may be aided in the difficult task of assessing guilt by the coaching, challenge, and support of other veterans, a therapist, or a wise pastoral caregiver. In assessing responsibility for a specific action, encourage a veteran to envision the total responsibility as a whole circle or pie. Draw a circle on a piece of paper and divide it into pie wedges and ask the veteran to apportion the responsibility for an incident to the various participants and entities.

"At the beginning of the battle, our tank caught on fire on the beach. I was the driver. We were sitting ducks, but we had to get out of there. The First Lieutenant and I were the only ones who survived. I only had a pistol, and for years I felt guilty that I didn't continue the attack. Years later I learned about survival guilt, and my counselor pointed out that the First Lieutenant had ordered me to stay hidden. All that helped me sort things out and let go of the guilt."

—WWII veteran

In the above example, the WWII veteran initially allotted the whole "guilt pie" to himself. With help from his counselor, he was able to see the largest piece of the pie went to the enemy who killed his buddies. Another small piece could be allotted to those who drew up the battle plan. It also helped him to realize that he was bound to obey his First Lieutenant's orders. The veteran's recognition of survivor guilt crystallized for him when he realized that guilt provided the motivation for his belief that he should have continued the attack with only a handgun.

Responses to guilt vary widely. Some veterans cannot admit the damage they have caused themselves or others. On the other hand, some believe that they deserve the feeling of guilt as punishment from God.

Confession and forgiveness. When the specific incidents producing feelings of guilt or remorse have been identified and responsibility has been assessed, a veteran is prepared to make a confession and receive forgiveness. Larry's story (next page)

KEY POINT
SURVIVOR GUILT

Survivor guilt occurs in most traumatic situations. Survivor guilt fuels depression and self-blame and can affect all relationships. The key feature of survivor guilt is to down play one's own survival with questions like "Why did I survive? Why didn't I die?" Soldiers, trained to watch out for each other, easily internalize guilt that belongs to the perpetrator or unavoidable misfortunes.

By helping the veteran properly assess responsibility, the caregiver relieves the veteran of unnecessary suffering induced by survivor guilt.

Another clue pointing to survivor guilt is the veteran who holds steadfastly to the perception that God is punishing him or her for what happened. Underpinning the guilt may be the belief that God punishes those who sin. Understanding the belief system of any sufferer can sometimes provide the key to relief from suffering.

Formal confession of survivor guilt can be harmful.

LARRY'S STORY

I want to say one thing about spirituality. This meant a lot to me. I went through this fifth step thing. Where you go to kind of a confession. Go talk to a minister. It doesn't have to be a minister. And that was a hard thing for me. I wasn't too thrilled. But, I thought, "I've got nothing to lose . . . what could happen? I'll give it a shot." Anyway you bring it all out and put it on the table. I had gone through a lot of garbage and I thought, "This can't be any worse than being tormented by this stuff."

So, I made some notes, and I sat down with this guy.

This guy was a Lutheran minister who had done AA fifth steps. So I thought, "This shouldn't be too bad . . . he must have heard some tough stuff from the AA people. It shouldn't be too bad."

So, I was telling him this stuff. It was an emotional thing. I'm choking this stuff out from Vietnam, from childhood, stuff I had done in my life that I was so ashamed of.

And, it was gut wrenching. After I got done he asked, "You ever talk with anyone about this stuff before?" And some of it I had, so I said, "Yeah." And he asked, "What did they say?" I said, "They told me you gotta forgive yourself, accept and love yourself." Did it work for you? "No, not really," I said. "I don't even like myself."

I thought, "It would be nice if I had that power, if I could tap myself on the head and love myself and forgive myself and turn myself into this wonderful person." But, I hadn't been able to do it for myself for 30 years. And I didn't expect I was going to be able to do it tomorrow. But, that's the whole basis for AA. You reach the point where you realize you need help.

And that pastor guy said, "You know, God loves you when you can't love yourself, and God forgives you, even when you can't forgive yourself." I don't know if I'd ever heard that before. Maybe I did. But, that time it sunk in. I finally understood that this was more than something I could do. I thought, "This makes sense that God forgives. It makes sense because it's something that I can't do for myself."

There was a peacefulness inside me, and something actually did happen. I still have mixed feelings about God and religion and the rest of this stuff. But, that was a moment in time where I thought, "Well, this is beyond me. God was doing something I can't do because I can't do it." But, I think that for any veteran that's got that kind of stuff, it's important to have the reassurance that God's forgiveness is there . . . for them too.[26]

captures the power and essence of confessional conversation and forgiveness.

Responses of persons on hearing words of forgiveness will vary. Some experience immediate and profound relief. Others may sense the full responsibility and consequences of their actions and for the first time experience profound sadness and remorse. Most people experience both reactions. Offer reassurance that these responses are normal. Confessional conversation can leave a person feeling renewed and refreshed, but also very vulnerable. Remind the veteran that emotional vulnerability often follows such disclosure and encourage the veteran to take good care of him or herself in the ensuing hours. Confessional conversation, whether informal or formal, is not meant to be a one-time fix, but rather a spiritual exercise to be repeated as memories and awareness unfold. Conclude by offering a prayer and blessing especially after a formal rite of confession and forgiveness.

Making Amends

For some, making amends can be the most important phase in spiritual healing. When veterans are ready, many find added relief from grief, guilt, and remorse if they are able to do something positive to offset wrongs done. In instances where making direct amends to the harmed persons may be impossible, misunderstood, or harmful, explore other creative ways to make amends. Here are some examples:

- Provide support to the family of a buddy who was killed or wounded.

- Connect with an organization formed by service members to make reparations or support refugees and injured citizens.

- Provide an anonymous gift to someone hurt or harmed.

- Consecrate or memorialize an activity or project in honor of someone. Sometimes this is best done anonymously.

Summary

In the many biblical post-resurrection stories, the Crucified Christ always presents himself to the traumatized disciples as a calm, peaceful, accepting, and forgiving presence. He does not condemn

---

CAREGIVER ALERT

Be prepared to help the veteran consider the difference between forgiving and forgetting. While few people who undergo significant trauma ever completely forget what happened, forgiveness is a free gift. In unbundling forgiving and forgetting, veterans may be liberated from the idea that they have to accomplish the impossible task of forgetting what happened so that they can be forgiven.

"I'm a Christian, and I was in therapy group. I finally got my main blockbuster out. For a while I was a pile of snot and tears. When I composed myself, someone made a joke and we all laughed. Then there was a moment of silence, and one of the guys in the group looked directly at me and just made the sign of the cross. From that moment, I knew God forgave me."

—Vietnam veteran

CLERGY ALERT

Most denominations have rites for individual confession and forgiveness. In the Roman Catholic tradition, the sacrament of reconciliation is administered by a priest. In most other traditions, the rite may be administered by a pastor or another spiritual caregiver. Some degree of preparation is necessary and the veteran will probably need some coaching before participating in the rite. Preparation includes awareness of wrongs experienced, some understanding of one's own responsibility, and readiness to admit mistakes. Clergy and caregivers need to prepare, too. Re-acquaint yourself with the rite and learn how it facilitates forgiveness and reconciliation.

those who were complicit in his killing. Rather, he accepts and forgives those who failed him in his hour of deepest need. And when the time is right, he offers them the opportunity to make amends by reinstating them to a similar ministry of peace and reconciliation. We are called to go and do likewise.

As people of faith, our human stories are wrapped in the Gospel's larger narrative of hope and healing. The scriptural healing narratives reveal profound connections among the physical, emotional, mental, relational, and spiritual aspects of our human story and God's compassion for the human family. If you tug at any aspect of human life, you also tug at the mysterious web of life that connects us all to the very heart of God.

The Church, in particular, should strive to be a safe place where hope and healing can take place. Pastors, parish nurses, and ministry teams are uniquely positioned for offering a healing ministry to people traumatized by war. Like returning soldiers, we all need to make sense of our experiences, confess our sins, receive forgiveness, and learn to live in a right relationship with God, self, and others.

The service member's return home begins with a warm welcome and the beginning of a serious transition. For them, coming home signals the opportunity for renewing, rebuilding, and restoring relationships with family, friends, church, and community. "Return" literally turns us all around and reconnects us to our deepest hopes, values, and dreams. Ultimately, through forgiveness and reconciliation, we return to God, no matter what the source of our alienation.

Chapter Six shows how the predictable ongoing cycles of the traditional church year provide a reliable framework of healing and renewal for service members and their families.

CAREGIVER NOTES

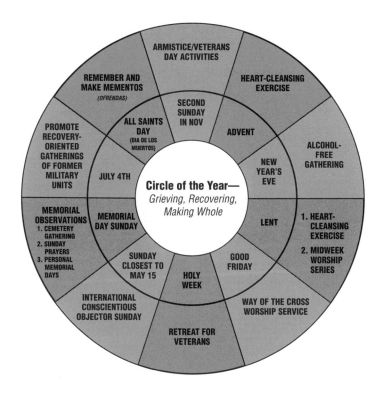

Circle of the Year— *Grieving, Recovering, Making Whole*

- ARMISTICE/VETERANS DAY ACTIVITIES
- HEART-CLEANSING EXERCISE
- SECOND SUNDAY IN NOV
- ADVENT
- ALCOHOL-FREE GATHERING
- NEW YEAR'S EVE
- 1. HEART-CLEANSING EXERCISE / 2. MIDWEEK WORSHIP SERIES
- LENT
- WAY OF THE CROSS WORSHIP SERVICE
- GOOD FRIDAY
- HOLY WEEK
- RETREAT FOR VETERANS
- INTERNATIONAL CONSCIENTIOUS OBJECTOR SUNDAY
- SUNDAY CLOSEST TO MAY 15
- MEMORIAL DAY SUNDAY
- MEMORIAL OBSERVATIONS 1. CEMETERY GATHERING 2. SUNDAY PRAYERS 3. PERSONAL MEMORIAL DAYS
- JULY 4TH
- PROMOTE RECOVERY-ORIENTED GATHERINGS OF FORMER MILITARY UNITS
- ALL SAINTS DAY (DIA DE LOS MUERTOS)
- REMEMBER AND MAKE MEMENTOS (OFRENDAS)

THE CHURCH'S ROLE #3

Provide Healing Rituals Throughout the Church Year

Twelve Spiritual Exercises for Use During the Church Calendar Year

Healing from the wounds of war can be a long, slow, and difficult process that takes place over time. Congregational spiritual exercises, activities, and rituals, practiced over the years, create a climate of healing and communicate a strong sense of solidarity with all those recovering from the wounds of war.

For example, theologian Dr. John Zemler, a former artillery captain, has suffered from PTSD and chronic pain since the 1980s. He suffered repetitive nightmares, which he called "screamers," for decades and only experienced their cessation after he told his painful story publicly in a religious setting. He speaks of the solace of "living the liturgy," seeing one's own story unfolding in the church calendar cycles of the lectionary. He attributes this personal immersion in the Biblical stories as the reason he can go on living.[27]

The following spiritual exercises, corresponding to the cycle of the church year, address the need for on-going healing and restoration.

Some, like the Advent heart-cleansing ritual, are designed for families. Others facilitate individual healing. Some address the need for re-integration into church and society. Feel free to adapt the following ideas to your own context.

1. Advent Heart-Cleansing Ritual— November or December

KEY POINT

For family reconciliation to occur, parents need to have a handle on their own issues before undertaking this exercise. Heavy, unresolved issues can sabotage the goal of family unity.

This healing ritual helps restore family cohesion by bringing family members together to experience acceptance, forgiveness, comfort, and support for losses incurred during separation. Unidentified, unshared, and ungrieved losses increase the pain of loneliness and separation, which often persists long after the service member has returned home. Advent is traditionally a time when Christians prepare to receive Christ by identifying and letting go of obstacles that separate us from God and from one another.

Purpose

- Gain insight and understanding into family members' experiences and feelings as they identify and name specific losses incurred during separation.

- Provide a safe context where family members can express their feelings.

- Offer acceptance, comfort, and support.

- Experience peace and reconciliation as family members forgive and welcome one another in the Spirit of Christ.

Process

1. Find a time when family members can gather together, perhaps after dinner. (Note: a family may prefer to meet in the church.)

2. Assign leadership roles, especially in families with children of various ages,

3. Arrange chairs in a circle and distribute pencils and several slips of paper to each family member.

4. One family member begins with the opening prayer.

Opening Prayer
God, we turn to you in our desire to heal and grow together as a family. We want to celebrate the love that comes to us at the birth of Jesus. Help us let go of obstacles in our relationships so that we can trust and enjoy each other this Christmas. Amen.

5. Light a candle.

6. Instruct family members to write down or draw a picture of losses and disappointments that occurred during separation. Small children will need help naming their feelings and recording them. Example: I felt sad that Dad missed my birthday.

7. Allow quiet time to write and draw.

8. Go around the circle as each person shares. Listen attentively while others speak and give everyone a chance to talk. Adults need to guard against over-processing their feelings in front of the children.

9. The veteran might want to go last and might offer responses to what others have said. Example: "I am sorry that I missed your birthday. That was hard for me, too."

10. Go around the circle again, giving each person an opportunity to say, "I let go of my disappointments and losses." Then place the papers in a fire-safe container.

11. After a brief moment of silence, the leader offers a confessional prayer.

Prayer
God, please help us let go of our sorrows and forgive each other so we can grow closer together as a family. Amen.

12. Using the flame from the ceremonial candle, an older family member sets fire to the slips of paper while others watch in silence. *Consider using a fireplace or moving the group to an outdoor fire pit or grill. This will prevent the fire alarm from going off.*

13. After the paper has burned, offer a closing prayer.

Closing Prayer
Dear God, we let go of our hurts. You know how we love and need each other and want to be family together. Help us feel your great love this Advent season. We thank you that we are able to be together. Now, help us to welcome Jesus, and each other with ready, open hearts. In Jesus' name we pray. Amen.

14. Extinguish the candle.

15. Conclude with hugs (or a group hug) and refreshments.

Special Considerations. When and if old feelings continue to crop up, encourage the family to reaffirm their commitment to accept those feelings and learn from their experiences.

Occasionally, a family member may want to talk to a friend, pastor, or counselor about feelings or reactions to this ritual.

Variation. Invite several families to gather at the church. A caregiver facilitates as each family group meets in a separate space, then joins with the others outside for the burning ceremony. When it concludes, gather all together as a large group for play, conversation, and refreshments.

2. New Year's Eve Gatherings— December 31st

Many veterans struggle with sobriety but want to celebrate the holidays with everyone else. Consider hosting an alcohol-free New Year's Eve event at the church or in a home.

Purpose

- Provide an alcohol-free, festive social gathering for veterans and their families.

- Reinforce connections between events of the past and the present—and good intentions for the future.

Process

1. Gather for a brief meditation with time for remembering the past, those departed or far away, and for offering reflection on present realities and future hopes and affirmations.

2. Allow time for each to express appreciation for those who have sacrificed on our behalf and especially for those who continue to struggle with the consequences of war.

3. Share in the preparation of food and participate together in activities to usher in the New Year.

3. Lenten Heart-Cleansing Ritual—February or March

Repeat the Advent Heart-Cleansing ritual during the Lenten season, with a special focus on those memories, regrets, and actions for which one seeks forgiveness from God, self, and others.

4. Lenten Midweek Worship Series—How To Be a People of Faith in a Time of War

Traditionally, Lent is a time for personal and communal repentance as people turn and return to God. Pastor Susan Tjernehoj and Christ Lutheran Church in St. Paul, Minnesota, developed the following midweek Lenten worship series to address the personal and communal spiritual wounds and brokenness of war. This worship series offers powerful testimony regarding the Church's capacity to bring hope and healing amidst the most challenging circumstances. The process described below is based on Christ Lutheran Church's series format.[28] If you wish to adopt this format, plan the event very carefully, use discernment in selecting participants to avoid exposing war survivors to unnecessary stress, and be sure each participant understands the purpose and expectations for his or her part in the worship service.

Purpose

- Call upon a congregation's capacity to facilitate healing by telling and hearing stories of the personal effects of war.

- Bring help, healing, and reconciliation to the church and community. Worship is a public event open to all in the community.

This worship is a spiritual exercise that models care and concern for everyone in the community in times of war.

Process

1. A series of midweek Lenten services are scheduled to allow time for sharing personal stories related to the experience of war. Communicate the design and purpose of the Lenten series to congregants ahead of time.

2. The pastor invites two or three members of the church (not limited to combat veterans) to speak briefly at each midweek Lenten service. These people already have a relationship of trust with the pastor and other members of the congregation.

3. Ask participants to offer brief responses to the following questions:

   When, where, and in what capacity did you experience war?

   What role did your faith play?

   How has this experience changed your understanding of God, Jesus, yourself, the Church?

   What wisdom would you give us who continue to be a community of faith in a time of war?

4. Let people know when they will speak. Ask them to keep their presentation to about three or four minutes.

5. Christ Lutheran Church used the evening prayer liturgy from their hymnal to frame the presentation.

Among those who spoke at Christ Lutheran Church were Afghanistan/Iraq veterans, a veteran from WWII, family members of a soldier killed in war, and people from other countries who had fled war as civilians. One group was composed of the children of parents who had been war refugees.

The following details on series planning offered by Pastor Tjernehoj may help you think through how to use the process in your own congregation.

People often need encouragement to tell their stories. Preface your request by openly acknowledging that living through war is a formative part of a person's life and point out how sharing their story can serve to strengthen the community. Offer the opportunity for conversation with the pastor before telling the story in church. This conversation may help prime the pump but should not lead to editing or prescribing any of the content.

Give people time to consider the invitation. A person may feel that it would be impossible to talk about his or her experiences. Not everyone will want to participate by sharing but may find relief in listening to others. Others may not feel comfortable being present. Just make the invitation and trust the internal wisdom of people to make a decision that is right for them.

It takes courage to engage in public conversation about such personal matters. The willingness to be vulnerable challenges people of faith to listen with great care and respect. During the worship at Christ Lutheran, there were times a speaker would begin to cry but after a few moments was able to continue speaking. Without exception, sharing at such a meaningful level led to increased empathy and congregational care for one another. While some participants exceeded the allotted time, none of the services lasted more than 45 minutes. Sometimes the one who is sharing may find it helpful for a trusted person to stand alongside for support and to continue reading from a prepared script if necessary.

The stories told at Christ Lutheran Church were remarkable and memorable. The WWII veteran, telling his story for the first time, brought a Bible signed by President Franklin Roosevelt. The outcomes of his sharing affirmed the premise that telling the story not only strengthened those who dared speak, but those who had the courage to listen as well. This WWII veteran appreciated the opportunity to finally recall events that were becoming distant history. Recalling the war gave him a chance to refresh his own memory and let others hear a first-hand account.

Another parishioner was a survivor of Liberian civil war atrocities. Significant prior therapy from the Center for Victims of Torture made it possible for her to share part of her experiences. She explained:

> *"I didn't want to tell anybody about my life. Pastor Sue encouraged me. She told me the more you tell your story, the more it will be like a weight lifting in you, little by little. Things in life put a lot of weight on you. You don't have to carry the weight alone. I have grown strong even though I had the bad experience. I had words of encouragement from brothers and sisters in Christ. It really makes me strong to go on."*

5. Good Friday— Way of the Cross Service

Good Friday is the time in the church year when worshippers identify their "crosses" and place them in the healing context of Jesus' suffering and death. The Way of the Cross is a Good Friday worship service that invites veterans to find needed rest and healing from the hurts and losses of war. The following suggestions for a Way of the Cross service reflect a blending of religious traditions. Design a service in keeping with your community's practices.

Purpose

- Identify and connect experiences of one's own suffering with the suffering of others.

- Sense that one's suffering is shared and carried by the communion of saints and borne by Jesus.

- Provide an opportunity to experience relief from the suffering caused by loneliness.

Process

1. Ideally, co-leadership for the service is provided by a veteran and a civilian.

2. The stations of the cross adapted for use in this liturgy are: 1) Jesus agonizes in the garden; 2) Jesus is condemned to death; 3) Jesus takes up his cross; 4) Jesus falls; 5) Mary encounters Jesus; 6) The cross is laid on Simon of Cyrene; 7) Jesus is stripped of his garments; 8) Jesus is crucified; 9) "Father, forgive them, for they know not what they do;" 10) Jesus promises paradise; 11) "Why hast thou forsaken me?" 12) Jesus dies on the cross.

3. Participants walk from station to station and a group liturgy is spoken at each station. See **www.welcomethemhomebook.com** to find one version of the Way of the Cross service. Service location depends on a number of variables, including number of participants, their walking abilities, and the weather. The Way of the Cross service can be held in a church sanctuary, the church grounds, in a cemetery, or even in the neighborhood.

4. If possible or desired, place artwork or artifacts at each station. You may consider placing photographs of congregants in the military or other symbols that co-mingle their suffering with the stations of the cross.

5. A processional cross or a rough-hewn cross carried by one of the participants may lead the procession. When held in the sanctuary, dim the lights and use meditative music. The service normally concludes in the sanctuary with the procession of the cross.

6. Offer a time for conversation and refreshments after the service.

Variation: During Lent, in preparation for Good Friday, invite veterans to journal about their experiences and memories as they relate to Jesus' stations of the cross.

6. Holy Saturday Retreat for Veterans

Holy Week can be a meaningful time for veterans to gather for a retreat patterned on the liturgy. The three days from Maundy Thursday to the Vigil of Easter are particularly poignant as we symbolically journey with Christ through his passion. On Maundy Thursday, we remember what it means to serve as Christ washes feet and communes with his disciples. On Good Friday, we visit the stations of the cross, suffering and dying with Christ as He descends to be with us in our hells. With Him we endure suffering and death, and on the Vigil of Easter we rise again in the waters of baptism, reaffirming what it means to be God's servant people on earth. On retreat, veterans engage their spiritual questions: "What wisdom can come from my suffering?" Those in transition may ask: "I'm no longer what I was, but I no longer know who I am. What parts of me are still in the tomb? Can I hope for resurrection?"

Purpose

- Use the liturgical power of Holy Week and community worship to facilitate healing and transformation.

- Provide a healing community for veterans.

Process

1. Plan a retreat beginning after Good Friday worship, through the Vigil of Easter, facilitated by a trusted caregiver, pastor, spiritual director, or counselor.

2. After Good Friday worship gather at the church or off-site in a retreat setting. The length of the retreat may vary, extending late into Friday night or continuing through Holy Saturday.

3. Consider beginning with Holy Communion and rejoining the congregation for worship at either the Vigil of Easter or Easter Day.

4. Use veterans' images and experiences as connections to the Way of the Cross service.

5. Activities and topics may include:

   - sharing recent dreams, especially from Good Friday night;

   - engaging in a brief physical work project;

   - journaling and talking about one's journaling;

   - using art as expression: wood, prose or poetry, natural objects, music, ceramics, paint, or drums;

   - writing a lament using Psalm 22, "My God, my God, why have you forsaken me?" as a template;

   - centering prayer and meditation;

   - sitting in solitude or in a natural setting; hermitage with a question or an assigned scripture passage;

   - receiving a massage or other specialized mind/body/energy work;

   - sharing meals;

   - engaging in story-telling around a fire.

7. International Conscientious Objector Day— Sunday Closest to May 15th

On International Conscientious Objector Day, we remember and appreciate people of all nations who resist war as a statement of their conscience. We remind ourselves of the Nuremberg principle:

> *"Individuals have international duties which transcend the national obligations of obedience. Therefore individual citizens have the duty to refuse to obey domestic laws to prevent crimes against peace and humanity from occurring."*
>
> —Nuremberg War Crime Tribunal, 1950

The United Nations has recognized that persons already performing military service may develop conscientious objections based on their experiences. Church authorities have long argued that an individual can conscientiously object to a particular war or act within a war, without being opposed to war in all forms. The church definition of conscientious objection includes both the obligation and right of a Christian to follow his/her own conscience in regard to particular circumstances.

Purpose

- Honor our spiritual obligation to reflect on the 'justness' of what government asks us to do.

- Remind people of faith about the sacred right and obligation to follow their conscience, regardless of civil law.

- Acknowledge our reliance on a Power that transcends earthly power and politics.

- Remember that the church supports those who follow their conscience when they are in conflict with directives of authorities or governments.

Process

1. Lift up the peace-making mandate of scripture during the Sunday worship service.

2. Honor people of faith who followed their conscience in refusing to wage unjust war.

3. Honor members of the military who stopped their comrades from killing civilians.

4. Educate people on local, national, and international peace efforts (e.g. "Decade of Non-violence").

8. Memorial Day—End of May

Memorial Day is a national holiday featuring military rituals and civic services to commemorate those who made great sacrifices for their country. Many communities hold Memorial Day parades, picnics, and ceremonies. Many rural churches with cemeteries celebrate with a religious or civic ceremony. The act of remembering within the Church carries with it deeply meaningful and necessary acts of grieving. Remembering reminds us that God helps us put back together the broken pieces of our lives. Memorial Day can be a very solemn day for veterans of recent combat and may awaken fresh feelings of grief and regret. Gather a group of church members together to attend the community Memorial Day events as a show of solidarity with veterans in the congregation. Those invited to be speakers and those planning civic ceremonies should be asked to keep the purposes for the commemorations in mind.

Purpose

- Share the burden of those who have gone to war.

- Be reminded of the losses from hostile forces, the war, and its aftermath.

- Grieve with veterans, loved ones, and friends.

Prayers for the Sunday Before Memorial Day

Consider including congregational petitions and prayers for all who have experienced war and long for peace.

Petition: We hold in our hearts those who continue to endure the trauma of war. We remember the maimed and the wounded. We remember those whose sleep is disturbed by the memories of war. We remember those who wrestle with addiction and those who struggle with depression. We especially remember those who have died (read names). Grant us patience and perseverance as we renew our pledge to support those in our midst who still suffer the trauma of war.

Petition: We hold in our hearts family members and loved ones who grieve and continue to suffer as a consequence of war. As a community of faith, use us to support them in the months and years ahead.

Petition: We pray for our enemies, the wounded and maimed, those who have died, and those who continue to grieve and suffer the traumatic consequences of war. We pray for civilians whose homes and livelihoods have been destroyed and the millions of refugees caught in the cross fire of war.

Confessional Prayer: As a nation, help us to realize and confess the role we play in causing the horrendous sufferings of war. Give us courage to bear responsibility for the things we have done and the things we have left undone, and give us wisdom to make amends that lead to justice, peace, and reconciliation.

9. Veterans' Personal Memorial Days

Veterans have personal memorial days indelibly etched in their own memories—the day a friend was killed, the day a buddy was wounded, or a day when their unit suffered casualties. Those dates may trigger an intense anniversary reaction. Sometimes anniversary reactions occur without the person's conscious awareness. A person may feel blue or angry and not know why. In this exercise encourage veterans to be intentional about remembering their significant dates and to develop a simple plan to memorialize those days.

Purpose

- Create awareness of unconscious grief.

- Promote a sense of control by developing a plan to grieve and receive comfort by memorializing the day.

- Prevent unnecessary adverse anniversary reactions.

Process

1. Encourage veterans to memorialize intentionally the events of a personal memorial day by journaling, writing a poem, planting a tree, writing a song, painting a picture, or spending the day with a trusted friend or in solitude and private contemplation.

2. Ask them to take one of the lament psalms, e.g. Psalm 69 or 88 as a model, and write their own personal lament.

3. Many Latinos/Latinas create *ofrendas* on the Day of the Dead *(Dia de los Muertos)*—a physical memorial to the recently deceased. Sometimes a shoebox can be decorated with pictures and memorabilia to honor a personal memorial day. (See *Dia de los Muertos*, Exercise #11, for more details.)

4. Pastors might consider making a phone call or sending a note expressing support and offering prayer on a significant day.

10. Independence Day—July 4

While not a church holiday, July 4 focuses on national values that provide meaning for soldiers fighting in war: independence, freedom, and love of country. This is a good time to encourage the reunion of military units for the purpose of mutual recovery from the wounds of war. The church or a small group within the church might consider hosting a lunch for those gathering at a nearby park.

Purpose

- Engage in an interactive healing process by helping veterans gather with people with whom they share a life-defining experience.

- Focus as community on shared values.

- Provide opportunity for fun, food, and sharing.

Process

1. Locate a recreational setting for a July 4th picnic or celebration.

2. Congregational members can assist with hospitality.

3. Design creative parades and ceremonies and decorate cakes.

4. Choose celebrative activities other than firework displays that do not have the potential to trigger flashbacks.

11. All Saints Day or *Dia de los Muertos*—First Sunday in November

All Saints Day was designated early in Christian history to remember those who have died in the faith. People of Latino descent may celebrate the *Dia de los Muertos* (Day of the Dead).

Purpose

- Connect us to our humanity and patterns of life and death.

- Remind us of our unity with those who have died in faith.

- Make *ofrendas* to connect people to their dearly departed, honor veterans and their families, and process grief as they remember those who have died.

- Learn to accept death as part of the larger circle of life.

- Celebrate the lives of those who have died.

Process

1. Check on which date Latinos in your community observe *Dia de los Muertos*.

2. Provide structure and opportunity for individuals or family groups to make personal *ofrendas*.

3. Providing flowers for the *ofrendas* is always appreciated. The *ofrendas* could be displayed in the hospitality area of the church or kept at home. The mood should be festive and should celebrate life.

4. At the All Saints Day Sunday service, read the names of those who have died in the previous year. Provide opportunity for members of the congregation to name those who have died as a result of the recent wars.

12. Armistice/Veterans Day (November 11) / Armistice/ Veterans Day Sunday (Second Sunday in November)

In 1918 Armistice Day was designated to commemorate the end of hostilities in World War I, the "war to end all wars." In 1954, the name was changed to Veterans Day to recognize the great sacrifices of veterans and their families and rededicate our national efforts to the cause of world peace. Commemorations at this time will be especially meaningful as the number of returning service members continue to increase.

Purpose

- Recall that Armistice Day is a dedication to the cause of world peace.

- Lament our failure, despite the sacrifices of previous wars, to learn to live in peace.

- Lament the sacrifices of war veterans and their families.

- Facilitate healing as the congregation shares in the burdens of suffering related to war.

Process

1. Engage a small group of veterans and civilians to plan the event.

2. Observe the traditional two minutes of silence at 11 a.m.

3. Read the list of those who have died, who are missing in action from past wars, or whose lives were destroyed by war, tolling a bell after each name.

4. Use any of the following liturgical elements in your Armistice/Veterans Day Sunday worship service.

Call to Worship: Today is Veterans Day, originally called Armistice Day in 1918 when Americans commemorated the end of World War I, understood then to be "the war to end all wars." We want to honor those who have endangered their lives in their desire to protect their country. We grieve with those who lost loved ones in the war and rejoice with those who returned home safely. We remember men and women who are even now in places of great danger in service to their country, and we pray for their deliverance. We pray for the day when there will be no more war. With these thoughts in our minds we come to worship this Veterans Day. God bless our time together.

Confession: Loving God, as the years of human history go by, we continue to bring suffering to each other through the scourge of war. We confess that we have too often sent our finest young men and women into fields of battle. We confess our complicity in raining death and destruction upon those we call enemy and the harm experienced by those we send. We confess that we seem to be unable to free ourselves from this pattern of death. Forgive us, Oh God. Forgive us, we pray.

Absolution: Gracious God, You know our frailties and grieve our warring madness. Remind us, each

and every one, that nothing can separate us from the love of God in Christ Jesus. God calls us to be children of God and, indeed, that is what we are. Though surrounded by war, live in peace! And may the peace of God, which surpasses all human understanding, keep your hearts and minds in Christ Jesus, now and forever. Amen.

Petitions: Prince of Peace, move the hearts and wills of those who govern to seek swift and just solutions in those places where violence and war hold sway. Shield the innocent, protect those who serve in the armed forces, grant patience to those who wait, comfort those who mourn. Empower us to be peacemakers in every arena of our lives. Lord, in your mercy, hear our prayer.

Healing Throughout the Year

Christian liturgy and the year-long cycle of the seasons within the church calendar contain powerful resources for hope and healing. As we live the liturgy throughout the church year, we experience continued reassurance of God's grace and presence in our lives. We learn to trust others, to bind the wounds, to return to God, and to grow in grace. Build your family life and your worship on the dependable strength of this rhythmic cycle for the benefit of all in church and community.

Afterword

Dear Reader,

We invite you to help create a culture of healing amidst a culture of violence. Having read this booklet, you are now invited to join the company of a small but growing number of people of faith willing to address *the hidden war after the war*.

You are now aware of a grim reality—that the aftermath of war diminishes the lives of many veterans and their families. Most of our service members do not seek or receive treatment for their post-war mental and spiritual problems. Of those who do, only a small minority receive adequate care. A purple heart or medal of honor cannot heal a wounded soul or violated conscience. Caregivers risk burnout and vicarious pain as they walk with people through traumatic experiences and memories.

We know, however, that with good support and timely interventions, healing occurs. Many veterans go on to live abundant lives and can become sources of healing and wisdom for others.

Service members and their families should not have to face the challenge of healing from the horror and evils of war alone. You have the life-giving resources and support of a faith community to join in this healing work. The Church, made bold and confident by God's redemptive love for us in Jesus Christ, is empowered to confront our deepest separation from God, self, and others that results from war.

We urge you to move forward in your efforts to create and sustain communities of faith, hope, and healing for veterans and their families as God gives you ability and strength to do so.

We are all on a path of transformation as we ask for God's help in healing the wounds of war. We humbly join veterans and their families in a recovery process that leads to spiritual health and a more abundant life. We look forward to the day when our country will have developed a strong, interactive network of faith-based caregivers skilled in the healing arts of recovery after war. We hope you will become part of the healing process and we trust that our collective efforts will be pleasing to God.

For I am convinced, that neither death, nor life, nor angels, nor rulers, nor things present, nor things to come, nor powers, nor height, nor depth, nor anything else in all creation, will be able to separate us from the love of God in Christ Jesus our Lord.

—Romans 8:38-39

CAREGIVER NOTES

Appendix A
Making a Referral: Accessing Veterans Administration and Community Resources for Veterans

Making an effective referral can be a complex, challenging task. Yet, it is so essential. Once you have heard and understood the needs of service members and their families, you may need to help them connect with additional resources and professional providers with specific expertise. This can be a daunting undertaking. Even experienced veterans' benefits coordinators are confused by the large number of available services and benefit options.

Remember that when people are in pain and anxiety they will have difficulty sorting through confusing options. They often have a hard time actively speaking up for themselves. At times like this, they are never at their best. If navigating the benefits maze is tiresome for professionals who work within these systems all the time, imagine how average veterans and their family members feel when they try to find help. The barriers of bureaucracy and red tape can be overwhelming. And in the end, the veteran often decides it's just not worth it. Making an effective referral may test the limits of your patience, endurance, and expertise. Never forget, however, that everyone needs a strong advocate who will walk with them when they are hurting.

Pastors, parish nurses, or other community caregivers can be extremely helpful in the referral process. Pastors often advocate for their members in many different settings. Service providers pay more attention to the patient when an advocate is present. Pastors and parish nurses are uniquely qualified to become veterans' advocates and to facilitate referrals. Just remember to be determined, tenacious, and polite—after all, the service providers you are speaking with are probably already overwhelmed themselves.

Asking for help is always a risk for anyone who is struggling. Your first step in being of assistance to veterans and their family members is to establish trust when they reach out to you for help. For service members and their families, who are trained to be tough at all times, reaching out takes a great deal of courage. They do not want to be shuffled around, referred to someone else, or promised a return call that never comes. Establish trust by assisting the service member or family to the best of your abilities before referring them on to another source of help.

When you do refer them to another source of help, be sure to follow up with each individual to make sure that the referral source matches the person's need. Don't let a person fall through the cracks. Check back. Ask, "How did it go?" "Did you get an appointment?" "Did it help?" "Do you think you might need a different kind of assistance?" Be encouraging, and if they at times find themselves short of hope, let them lean on you and borrow some of yours! Assure them that while you cannot deliver the cure, you will be there with them until they find the help they need.

Professional Sources of Help

The following professional options are divided into three groups; Veterans Administration (VA) services, local civilian care providers, and other national resources.

Accessing Veterans Administration Services

The Department of Veterans Affairs (VA) is the primary benefit source for all veterans. Veterans should notify the VA of their eligibility for services as soon as they return from a deployment. Failure to contact the VA within the proper time period can result in lack of financial support and access to services.

The main purpose of the VA is to provide care for veterans. Generally, family members are not eligible for benefits. Therefore the VA is not normally an appropriate solution for family members needing assistance. However, VA staff will often make excellent suggestions for other providers with proper experience who are available to help the family members. So, feel free to ask.

Department of Veterans Affairs

1-800-827-1000

www.va.gov

The VA website explains how to apply for health benefits, compensation, and vocational rehabilitation benefits.

CAREGIVER ALERT

Service members may not know that the National Defense Authorization Act (NDAA) signed into law on January 28, 2008, extends the period of enrollment for health care eligibility for discharged veterans who served in a theater of combat operations after November 11, 1998. Check to see if your service member is eligible.

State Veteran Centers

The VA website also contains a comprehensive directory of State Vet Centers. These centers provide readjustment counseling and outreach services to all veterans who served in any combat zone. Services are also available for family members for military related issues. These services are provided at no cost to the veteran or family. To find the nearest State Vet Center, go to the VA website (**www.va.gov**) and click on LOCATIONS.

Some service members are not comfortable seeking direct care from the VA. For others, distance is a problem. Many prefer local civilian service providers.

Identifying Local Civilian Service Providers

Community-based professionals often play a vital role in the lives of veterans, particularly those who serve in the National Guard and Reserve (collectively referred to as Reservists). These veterans, a high percentage of those serving in the Iraq and Afghanistan wars, are non-traditional military, typically civilians living within civilian communities rather than living within self-contained military bases. They have civilian employment and are not career military. When called upon for active military duty, they may experience additional stressors such as losing a small business or having two parents called up to be deployed simultaneously. They also often find it more difficult to access VA and other military services once they return. Receiving care hundreds of miles from home is not feasible for many of these veterans and their families. Therefore, when the need arises, the civilian military service member often must find help through a local community provider.

Get to know the community-based providers in your area. You probably already know many of them from previous experience. Develop contacts with providers who understand the specific needs of the military service members within your community. Discover who has gained the practical skills for understanding the issues unique to the Reservist population. Civilian community providers can be a critical link in assisting veterans and their families during deployment and reintegration. Here are some suggestions you can use to strengthen that linkage.

1. Build your own network of trusted providers. Find out who is providing the best service in your area. Take time to meet with them, and get to know each of them. Referrals work better between colleagues who know one another and share a mutual respect. Remember to ask the provider if the military covers any or all of the cost of counseling. And always inquire about confidentiality.

2. As you seek out continuing education opportunities to help you better understand the military culture and the mental health problems caused by combat trauma, share this knowledge and understanding with your local colleagues and other community providers.

3. Make an effort to learn about other health providers in your community as well as the VA system and mental health services that are available through the VA. You could even take the initiative to schedule an educational seminar for your local ministerium or parish nurse group with speakers from local providers and the VA, who would describe their services and how you can help veterans access them.

4. Be aware of County Veterans Service Officers, Family Readiness Groups (FRG), or Family Assistance Centers (FAC) in your area. The military also provides FACs at various strategic geographic locations throughout each state. Volunteer military spouses operate FACs. Find your nearest FAC at: **www.guardfamily.org**

5. Identify the local groups who supply volunteer support services. Veterans themselves often start volunteer support services out of their strong commitment and passion to help other veterans. Seek out programs that provide veterans and their families with local community support, including veteran-to-veteran and family-to-family support outreach.

Discovering Other National Sources for Assistance and Referral

Community care providers should be aware that veterans and their families might be resistant to seeking care through the VA or other military-associated programs due to perceived limited confidentiality and stigma within the military. Several national programs are available that provide free and confidential service to military service members and their families.

Veterans Service Organizations

www1.va.gov/vso

The above link will take you to an extensive online directory of many organizations that serve veterans.

National Association of County Veteran Service Officers

www.nacvso.org

County Veteran Service Officers are tasked with assisting veterans in developing and processing their claims. The largest percentage of claims presented to the Veterans Administration each year originate in a county veterans office. This group helps speed the process of claims processing and the transition of military personnel to civilian life.

Military One Source

1-800-342-9647 or 1-888-755-9355

www.militaryonesource.com

Military One Source provides 24/7/365 access to information for service members and their families including areas of parenting and child care, personal and family readiness, education, midlife and retirement, disability, financial, legal, everyday issues, work, health, emotional well-being, addiction, and recovery. Counseling for grief, marital issues, stress, and adjustment to deployment are available at no cost to service members and their primary family members for up to 12 sessions per family member per incident or issue.

American Red Cross

www.redcross.org

This international, nonprofit organization offers support and comfort to military service members and their families, including a vital link for family members who need to contact their service members overseas in an emergency.

United Way

www.liveunited.org

The United Way is an instrumental organization for community-based outreach, funding, and resources. Some United Way organizations are developing specific resource lists of local services for veterans and their families. Go to the website. Plug in your zip code. Then call the local contact numbers provided.

The GI Rights Hotline

www.girightshotline.org

1-877-447-4487

The GI Rights Hotline is answered by a coalition of nonprofit, non-governmental organizations who provide information to members of the military about conscientious objection, discharges, grievance and complaint procedures, and other civil rights.

Once you have built a relationship of trust with the service member and the family, you do not have to feel the weight of providing all the care yourself. Know your limits and the limits of your congregation. Rely on other professionals to provide the care needed in the specific areas of their expertise. You are now a trusted advocate. Use your position and authority to help those in need identify and connect with the other professional services that can become most useful to them as they continue to move forward with their healing process.

Parish Nurse Screening Tools

Screening tools for PTSD, depression, and TBI can be used by primary care providers to help veterans more clearly identify the possible causes of their symptoms. Always use screening tools within the context of the relationship you have developed with the service member. Insure privacy when discussing symptoms and describe how a screening tool can be used as an *initial* step to accessing more comprehensive care. Discuss the results of the screening tool with the individual, and together decide how to access the best follow-up evaluation, if needed.

Primary Care Post-Traumatic Stress Disorder Screening Tool

Current research suggests that the results of the PC-PTSD should be considered positive if a person answers "yes" to any three (3) of the following items.

PRIMARY CARE PTSD SCREEN (PC-PTSD)

In your life, have you ever had any experience that was so frightening, horrible, or upsetting that in the past month you…		
1. have had nightmares about it or thought about it when you did not want to?	YES	NO
2. tried hard not to think about it or went out of your way to avoid situations that reminded you of it?	YES	NO
3. were constantly on guard, watchful, or easily startled?	YES	NO
4. felt numb or detached from others, activities or your surroundings?	YES	NO

CAREGIVER ALERT

A positive response to screening questions does not necessarily indicate that the person has the condition for which screening is being done. However, a positive response does indicate that a person may have trauma-related problems and further investigation of symptoms by a mental health professional is warranted.

An extended PTSD screening tool can be found at: *PTSD*. Weathers, F.W., Huska, J.A., Keane, T.M. PCL-M for DSM-IV. Boston: National Center for PTSD-Behavioral Science Division, 1991. Accessed September 2009 at **www.opq.med.va.gov/cpg/ptsd/ptsd_cpg/content/appendices/appendixc.htm**

For further information on screening for PTSD, see U.S. Department of Veterans Affairs National Center for Posttraumatic Stress Disorder (NCPTSD) at **www.ncptsd.va.gov**

Depression Screening

It is not uncommon for people who have returned from military service to experience symptoms of depression. Depression is not just feeling "down" for a short period of time. It is a medical condition that can be effectively treated.

Parish nurses, chaplains, and pastoral counselors can use the depression screening tool and instructions for use, found on pages 100 and 101, to determine whether further evaluation is needed.

KEY POINT

The depression screening tool is not diagnostic, but is designed to help the parish nurse, the chaplain, or the pastoral counselor decide if further evaluation or treatment would be helpful. A formal diagnosis of depression can only be made by a qualified mental health professional.

CAREGIVER ALERT

If the service member indicates any thoughts of suicide in question #9 of the Patient Health Questionnaire on the next page, you need to follow up immediately and ask if he or she has a plan. Remember, a thought-out plan usually indicates higher risk. It may be necessary to escort the person to a professional caregiver or facility or stay with him or her until help arrives and a care plan is established. (Refer to the suicide intervention protocol in the Caregiver Alert sidebar on page 37.)

PATIENT HEALTH QUESTIONNAIRE (PHQ-9)

NAME: _____   DATE:_____

Over the *last 2 weeks,* how often have you been
bothered by any of the following problems?
(use "✓" to indicate your answer)

	Not at all	Several days	More than half the days	Nearly every day
1. Little interest or pleasure in doing things	0	1	2	3
2. Feeling down, depressed, or hopeless	0	1	2	3
3. Trouble falling or staying asleep, or sleeping too much	0	1	2	3
4. Feeling tired or having little energy	0	1	2	3
5. Poor appetite or overeating	0	1	2	3
6. Feeling bad about yourself—or that you are a failure or have let yourself or your family down	0	1	2	3
7. Trouble concentrating on things, such as reading the newspaper or watching television	0	1	2	3
8. Moving or speaking so slowly that other people could have noticed. Or the opposite—being so fidgety or restless that you have been moving around a lot more than usual	0	1	2	3
9. Thoughts that you would be better off dead, or of hurting yourself in some way	0	1	2	3

add columns: [_____] + [_____] + [_____]

(Healthcare professional: For interpretation of TOTAL, please refer to accompanying scoring card).   **TOTAL:** [_____]

---

10. If you checked off *any* problems, how *difficult* have these problems made it for you to do your work, take care of things at home, or get along with other people?

Not difficult at all	_____
Somewhat difficult	_____
Very difficult	_____
Extremely difficult	_____

for doctor or healthcare professional use only

PHQ-9 QUICK DEPRESSION ASSESSMENT

For initial diagnosis:

1. Patient completes PHQ-9 Quick Depression Assessment.

2. If there are at least 4 ✓s in the two right columns (including Questions #1 and #2), consider a depressive disorder. Add score to determine severity.

3. *Consider Major Depressive Disorder*
   • if there are at least 5 ✓s in the two right columns (one of which corresponds to Question #1 or #2).

Consider Other Depressive Disorder
   • if there are 2 to 4 ✓s in the two right columns (one of which corresponds to Question #1 or #2).

Note: Since the questionnaire relies on patient self-report, all responses should be verified by the clinician, and a definitive diagnosis is made on clinical grounds, taking into account how well the patient understood the questionnaire, as well as other relevant information from the patient. Diagnoses of Major Depressive Disorder or Other Depressive Disorder also require impairment of social, occupational, or other important areas of functioning and ruling out normal bereavement, a history of a Manic Episode (Bipolar Disorder), and a physical disorder, medication, or other drug as the biological cause of the depressive symptoms.

To monitor severity over time for newly diagnosed patients or patients in current treatment for depression:

1. Patients may complete questionnaires at baseline and at regular intervals (eg, every 2 weeks) at home and bring them in at their next appointment for scoring or they may complete the questionnaire during each scheduled appointment.

2. Add up ✓s by column. For every ✓:

"Several days" = 1   "More than half the days" = 2   "Nearly every day" = 3

3. Add together column scores to get a TOTAL score.

4. Refer to accompanying PHQ-9 Scoring Card to interpret the TOTAL score.

5. Results may be included in patients' files to assist you in setting up a treatment goal, determining degree of response, as well as guiding treatment intervention.

PHQ-9 SCORING CARD FOR SEVERITY DETERMINATION

for healthcare professional use only

Scoring—add up all checked boxes on PHQ-9

For every ✓: Not at all = 0; Several days = 1;
More than half the days = 2; Nearly every day = 3

Interpretation of Total Score

Total Score	Depression Severity
0-4	None
5-9	Mild
10-14	Moderate
15-19	Moderately severe
20-27	Severe

Traumatic Brain Injury Screening Tool

The signs and symptoms of a traumatic brain injury (TBI) can be subtle and may not appear until days or weeks following the injury. Symptoms may also be missed entirely, as people may look fine even though they may act or feel differently than normal.

Available at **www.gao.gov/new.items/d08276.pdf**, the following verbally administered screening tool can be used to help identify mild TBI. If a veteran answers "yes" to one or more questions in each of the four sections, he or she has screened positive for a possible mild TBI. The VA directs providers to not diagnose a patient with a mild TBI based solely on the results of the TBI screening tool because it is possible to respond positively to all four sections and not have a mild TBI, due to the presence of conditions such as PTSD that present similar symptoms. The VA's policy requires that veterans who screen positive on the VA's TBI screening test should be further evaluated by a specialized health care provider who will be able to determine the presence and degree of TBI.

Section 1:
During any of your OEF/OIF deployment(s) did you experience any of the following events? (Check all that apply.)

❑ Blast or explosion

❑ Vehicular accident/crash (including aircraft)

❑ Fragment wound or bullet wound above shoulders

❑ Fall

If the veteran responses positively to any of the above items, ask the questions from Section 2:

Section 2:
Did you have any of these symptoms IMMEDIATELY afterwards? (Check all that apply)

❑ Losing consciousness/"knocked out"

❑ Being dazed, confused or "seeing stars"

❑ Not remembering the event

❑ Concussion

❑ Head injury

If a veteran experiences any of the effects in Section 2, proceed to Section 3.

Section 3:
Did any of the following problems begin or get worse afterwards? (Check all that apply)

❑ Memory problems or lapses

❑ Balance problems or dizziness

❑ Sensitivity to bright light

❑ Irritability

❑ Headaches

❑ Sleep problems

If the veteran has had any of the above symptoms, proceed to Section 4.

Section 4:
In the past week, have you had any of the symptoms from section 3? (Check all that apply)

❑ Memory problems or lapses

❑ Balance problems or dizziness

❑ Sensitivity to bright light

❑ Irritability

❑ Headaches

❑ Sleep problems

Appendix C

Wounds of War Assessment

This assessment will help you identify factors that may affect the health and well-being of veterans who have served in combat and thereby suffered wounds of war.

There are three sections to the inventory:

1) Specific war-related EXPERIENCES that may cause or contribute to health problems.

2) Emotional, physical, spiritual, relational, social, and occupational SYMPTOMS that may be related to health problems.

3) SELF-CARE strategies and professional TREATMENTS that may help prevent/relieve health problems or alleviate symptoms that many combat veterans suffer.

In each section, you will be asked to assess how your experience is related to nine different disease patterns that are frequently reported by veterans—sometimes years or decades following combat. These nine health problems are loosely grouped into three categories: physical/mental disease, combat-related difficulties, and spiritual maladies, represented by three columns on the right side of each chart.

PHYSICAL/MENTAL DISEASE

TBI = Traumatic Brain Injury

PTSD = Post-Traumatic Stress Disorder

Dep = Depression

COMBAT-RELATED DISEASE

COSR = Combat Operational Stress Reaction

MST = Military Sexual Trauma

SA = Substance Abuse

SPIRITUAL DISEASE

Grief = Grief

Soul = Soul Wounds

Con = Wounds of Conscience

© John Sippola, Chaplain, LTC, ret., MDiv; Amy Blumenshine, MSW, MA; Donald A Tubesing, PhD, MDiv; Valerie Yancey, PhD, RN

War-Related Experiences Inventory

Instructions

1. Read down the list of war-related events in the LEFT column and CHECK any you have experienced. If you have experienced any other traumatic events, write them in the blank spaces.

2. Go back, and for each item you checked, consider how the experience might be related to one or more of the nine potential health problems listed in the columns to the RIGHT. Where you see a possible connection, CIRCLE the Xs that seems to be related. For example, if you checked #9, "Witnessed the death of a buddy," you would most likely circle the X under "Grief." But you also might also circle the X under "Dep" (depression) or "SA" (substance abuse) if the event contributed to your depression or excessive use of alcohol or drugs.

You may be experiencing a health condition or problem that is not included in the "disease/difficulties/maladies" columns. For example, the death of a buddy might cause or contribute to panic attacks. If so, then you could add another column, label it "PA" (panic attacks) and mark where the two intersect.

PHYSICAL/MENTAL DISEASE	COMBAT-RELATED DISEASE	SPIRITUAL DISEASE
TBI = Traumatic Brain Injury	COSR = Combat Operational Stress Reaction	Grief = Grief
PTSD = Post-Traumatic Stress Disorder	MST = Military Sexual Trauma	Soul = Soul Wounds
Dep = Depression	SA = Substance Abuse	Con = Wounds of Conscience

Your war-related experience could cause ⟶	Physical/Mental Disease			Combat-Related Disease			Spiritual Disease		
WAR-RELATED EXPERIENCES	TBI	PTSD	Dep	COSR	MST	SA	Grief	Soul	Con
1. Fired upon		X	X	X		X	X	X	
2. Killed a soldier		X	X	X		X	X	X	X
3. Killed a child		X	X	X		X	X	X	X
4. Killed a woman		X	X	X		X	X	X	X
5. Mistakenly killed or wounded someone from one's own side		X	X	X		X	X	X	X
6. Survived a blast	X	X	X	X		X	X	X	
7. Blow to the head causing a concussion	X	X	X	X		X	X		
8. Witness severe wounding of a buddy		X	X	X		X	X	X	X
9. Witness death of a buddy		X	X	X		X	X	X	X
10. Sight of decomposing, mutilated bodies		X	X	X		X	X	X	X
11. Experienced the stench of dead bodies		X	X	X		X	X	X	X

continued

© John Sippola, Chaplain, LTC, ret., MDiv; Amy Blumenshine, MSW, MA; Donald A Tubesing, PhD, MDiv; Valerie Yancey, PhD, RN

Your war-related experience could cause ⟶	Physical/Mental Disease			Combat-Related Disease			Spiritual Disease		
WAR-RELATED EXPERIENCES *continued*	TBI	PTSD	Dep	COSR	MST	SA	Grief	Soul	Con
12. Handling dead bodies		X	X	X		X	X	X	
13. Witnessed or tried to rescue someone who died		X	X	X		X	X	X	X
14. Lived in constant danger of death or injury		X	X	X		X	X	X	
15. Constant worry of nuclear, chemical, biological attack		X	X	X		X	X	X	
16. Survived a bad accident	X	X	X			X	X		
17. Dehydration, heat stroke	X	X				X			
18. Sleep deprivation		X		X		X			
19. Witnessed or discharged a "mercy" killing		X	X	X		X	X	X	X
20. Destroyed someone's home or property		X	X	X		X	X	X	X
21. Witnessed or particpated in atrocities		X	X	X		X	X	X	X
22. Saw/participated in torture of soldiers, civilians, animals		X	X	X		X	X	X	X
23. Intentional killing of non-combatants		X	X	X		X	X	X	X
24. Physically assaulted enemy or fellow soldier		X	X	X		X	X	X	X
25. Was physically assaulted by enemy or a fellow soldier	X	X	X	X		X	X	X	X
26. Sexually assaulted someone		X	X	X		X	X	X	X
27. Being sexually assaulted		X	X	X	X	X	X	X	X
28. Being sexually harrassed		X	X	X	X	X	X	X	X
29. Fear of sexual assault		X	X	X	X	X	X	X	X
30. Sustained mild TBI	X	X	X	X		X	X		
31. Suffering from PTSD		X	X	X		X	X	X	X
32. Suffering from depression			X	X		X	X	X	
33. Suffering from combat operational related stress		X	X	X		X	X	X	X
34. Abusing substances (meds, alcohol, drugs, etc.)	X		X			X	X	X	X
35. Suffering from grief			X	X		X	X	X	X
36. Suffering from soul wounds		X	X	X		X	X	X	X
37. Suffering wounds of conscience		X	X	X		X	X	X	X
38. Exposure to toxins		X					X		

Wounds of War Symptoms Inventory

Instructions

1. Read down the list of emotional, physical (mind/body), spiritual, relational, social, and occupational SYMPTOMS in the LEFT column and CHECK any you have experienced recently. If you have noticed any other significant symptoms, write them in the blank spaces.

2. Go back, and for each item you checked, consider how the symptom might be related to one or more of the nine potential health problems listed in the columns to the RIGHT. Where you see a possible connection, CIRCLE the Xs that seems to be related.

PHYSICAL/MENTAL DISEASE	COMBAT-RELATED DISEASE	SPIRITUAL DISEASE
TBI = Traumatic Brain Injury	COSR = Combat Operational Stress Reaction	Grief = Grief
PTSD = Post-Traumatic Stress Disorder	MST = Military Sexual Trauma	Soul = Soul Wounds
Dep = Depression	SA = Substance Abuse	Con = Wounds of Conscience

Your symptoms may be related to ⟶	Physical/Mental Disease			Combat-Related Disease			Spiritual Disease		
WOUNDS OF WAR SYMPTOMS	TBI	PTSD	Dep	COSR	MST	SA	Grief	Soul	Con
Emotional Symptoms (Excessive and Persistent)									
1. Angry outbursts (excessive irritability)	X	X	X	X	X	X	X	X	X
2. Excessive sadness (tears)	X	X	X	X	X	X	X	X	X
3. Feeling lost	X	X	X	X	X	X	X	X	X
4. Extreme distrust	X	X	X	X	X	X	X	X	X
5. Feeling confused	X	X	X	X	X	X	X	X	X
6. Feeling unsafe	X	X	X		X	X		X	
7. Feeling alone	X	X	X	X	X	X	X	X	X
8. Feeling afraid (may also experience panic attacks)	X	X	X	X	X	X	X	X	X
9. Feeling awkward	X	X	X	X	X	X	X	X	X
10. Easily distracted	X	X	X		X	X			
11. Emotional shut down	X	X	X	X	X	X	X	X	X
12. Over-reactive	X	X		X	X	X	X		X
13. Heavy sense of guilt		X	X	X	X	X	X	X	X
14. Deep-seated shame		X	X	X	X	X	X	X	X
15. Loss of desire in hobbies, activities, sex	X	X	X	X	X		X		
16. Hopelessness and despair	X	X	X	X	X	X	X	X	X

continued

© John Sippola, Chaplain, LTC, ret., MDiv; Amy Blumenshine, MSW, MA; Donald A Tubesing, PhD, MDiv; Valerie Yancey, PhD, RN

106

Your symptoms may be related to ⟶	Physical/Mental Disease			Combat-Related Disease			Spiritual Disease		
WOUNDS OF WAR SYMPTOMS *continued*	TBI	PTSD	Dep	COSR	MST	SA	Grief	Soul	Con
17. Feeling worthless		X	X	X	X	X		X	X
18. Night terrors		X				X			X
19. Need for adrenalin rush		X		X					
Physical Symptoms (Mind / Body)									
1. Chronic headaches	X	X	X	X	X	X	X	X	X
2. Digestive problems	X	X	X	X	X	X	X	X	X
3. Disruption in sleep patterns	X	X	X	X	X	X	X	X	X
4. Sluggish thinking	X	X	X	X	X	X	X		
5. Memory loss or poor concentration	X	X	X	X	X	X	X		
6. Brief periods of unconsciousness	X								
7. Feeling unusually tired (chronic fatigue)	X	X	X	X	X	X	X	X	X
8. Sensory problems (blurred vision, loss of smell, ears ring)	X								
9. Dizziness / loss of balance	X			X		X			
10. Loss of executive functions (decision/problem solving)	X	X	X	X	X	X	X		
11. Self-medicating		X	X	X	X	X	X	X	X
12. Easily startled		X		X	X	X			
13. Unusual weight gain / loss			X		X				
14. Excessive sleeping, insomnia		X	X	X	X	X	X		
15. Nausea	X	X		X	X	X	X	X	X
16. Persistent thoughts of suicide			X		X	X	X	X	X
17. Loss of bowel / bladder control		X		X					
18. Suicidal thinking	X	X	X	X	X	X	X	X	X
Spiritual Symptoms									
1. Nothing matters (nihilism)	X	X	X	X	X	X	X	X	X
2. Ongoing moods of hopelessness or pessimism		X	X	X	X	X	X	X	X
3. Lack of peace of mind	X	X	X	X	X	X	X	X	X
4. Diminished capacity for joy	X	X	X	X	X	X	X	X	X
5. Diminished capacity to love one's self / neighbor	X	X	X	X	X	X	X	X	X
6. Loss of faith in God		X	X	X	X	X	X	X	X
7. Self-absorption	X	X	X	X	X	X	X	X	X
8. An ethic that says it is OK to target non-combatants		X	X	X		X	X	X	X

continued

© John Sippola, Chaplain, LTC, ret., MDiv; Amy Blumenshine, MSW, MA; Donald A Tubesing, PhD, MDiv; Valerie Yancey, PhD, RN

Your symptoms may be related to ——————————→	Physical/Mental Disease			Combat-Related Disease			Spiritual Disease		
Wounds of War Symptoms *continued*	TBI	PTSD	Dep	COSR	MST	SA	Grief	Soul	Con
9. Diminished sense of grace and gratitude	X	X	X	X	X	X	X	X	X
10. Believing that it is OK to dehumanize / torture people	X	X	X	X		X	X	X	X
11. Diminished sense of meaning and purpose in life	X	X	X	X	X	X	X	X	X
12. Diminished capacity to give and receive forgiveness	X	X	X	X	X	X	X	X	X
13. Diminished capacity to appreciate the good and beautiful	X	X	X	X	X	X	X	X	X
Relational, Social, Occupational Symptoms									
1. Self-imposed isolation		X	X	X	X	X	X		
2. Avoiding people, places, activities, thoughts, topics	X	X	X	X	X	X	X	X	X
3. Feeling disconnected from people	X	X	X	X	X	X	X	X	
4. Difficulty communicating	X	X	X	X	X	X	X		
5. Diminished parenting skills	X	X	X	X	X	X	X		
6. Diminished intimacy skills (communication)	X	X	X	X	X	X	X		
7. Problems with sexuality (communication / performance)	X	X	X	X	X	X	X		X
8. Difficulty learning and retaining	X	X	X	X	X	X	X		
9. Difficulty solving problems and making decisions	X	X	X	X	X	X	X		

KEY POINT

Exposure to toxins has been widespread in the last two wars, and exposure to toxins during deployment has been known to cause illness years later. Given the range of possible exposure, it is impossible to predict what the symptoms will be. Toxic exposures from past wars, however, have manifested as immune system disorders, chronic fatigue, cancer, reproductive problems, neurological problems, and diabetes. Any of these conditions can also cause behavioral problems, especially when undiagnosed. If perplexing health problems emerge, consider the possibility of military toxic exposure.

Self-Care Treatment Inventory

Instructions

1. Read down the list of SELF-CARE strategies and TREATMENTS in the LEFT column and CHECK any you have utilized to deal with your wounds of war. Feel free to add additional cares and cures.

2. Go back, and for each item you checked, consider which of the nine potential health problems listed in the columns to the RIGHT might have been positively affected by your action or seeking care. Where you see a possible connection, CIRCLE the Xs that seems to be related.

PHYSICAL/MENTAL DISEASE	COMBAT-RELATED DISEASE	SPIRITUAL DISEASE
TBI = Traumatic Brain Injury	COSR = Combat Operational Stress Reaction	Grief = Grief
PTSD = Post-Traumatic Stress Disorder	MST = Military Sexual Trauma	Soul = Soul Wounds
Dep = Depression	SA = Substance Abuse	Con = Wounds of Conscience

Your self-care and treatment may alleviate ⟶

SELF-CARE AND TREATMENTS	Physical/Mental Disease			Combat-Related Disease			Spiritual Disease		
	TBI	PTSD	Dep	COSR	MST	SA	Grief	Soul	Con
1. Adequate sleep and nutrition	X	X	X	X	X	X	X	X	X
2. Good support system (5 knowledgeable people who care)	X	X	X	X	X	X	X	X	X
3. Drug therapy (along with counseling)		X	X		X	X	X		
4. Psychotherapy		X	X	X	X	X	X	X	X
5. Spiritual care	X	X	X	X	X	X	X	X	X
6. Patient / family education	X	X	X	X	X	X	X	X	X
7. Family therapy		X	X	X	X	X	X	X	
8. Group therapy		X		X	X		X		
9. Relaxation therapies (yoga, massage, biofeedback, etc.)		X		X	X			X	
10. Anger management	X	X	X	X	X	X	X		
11. Pastoral care (life skills, forgiveness, acceptance)				X	X	X	X	X	
12. Cognitive-behavioral therapy		X	X		X	X			
13. Eye movement densitization and reprocessing (EMDR)		X			X	X			
14. Prayer practice (corporate / individual)	X	X	X	X	X	X	X	X	X
15. Meditation practice (centering prayer)		X	X	X	X	X	X	X	X
16. Regular connection with a caring community of faith	X	X	X	X	X	X	X	X	X

© John Sippola, Chaplain, LTC, ret., MDiv; Amy Blumenshine, MSW, MA; Donald A Tubesing, PhD, MDiv; Valerie Yancey, PhD, RN

Endnotes

1. "Returning Soldiers Come Up Short." *Duluth News Tribune* 28 Nov. 2007.

2. Bilmes, Linda J., and Joseph E. Stiglitz. *The Three Trillion Dollar War: The True Cost of the Iraq Conflict.* New York, NY: W.W. Norton Inc., 2008.

3. Tanielian, Terri, Lisa H. Jaycox, Terry L. Schell, Grant N. Marshall, M. Audrey Burnam, Christine Eibner, Benjamin R. Karney, Lisa S. Meredith, Jeanne S. Ringel, and Mary E. Vaiana. "Invisible Wounds: Mental Health and Cognitive Care Needs of America's Returning Veterans." *Rand Center for Military Health Policy Research.* www.rand.org/pubs/research_briefs/RB9336 (Accessed 3 Sept. 2009.)

4. Blumenshine, Amy. "Soldiers' Ongoing Sacrifices: The Challenge of Coming Home." *Caring Connections: An Inter-Lutheran Journal for Practitioners and Teachers of Pastoral Care and Counseling* (2007). www/ldr.org/resources/sacrifice.pdf

5. Tyson, Anne, and Josh White. "Strains to Remain Despite Shorter Tours, Say Gates, Mullen." *Washington Post* 11 Apr. 2008: AO4.

6. "Ex-military Marksman Shot Down Sheriff's Copter." *Sydney Morning Herald* 17 Aug. 2005.

7. Hoge, Charles W., Stephen C. Messer, and Carl A. Castro. "Combat Duty in Iraq and Afghanistan and Mental Health Problems and Barriers to Care." *New England Journal of Medicine* 351.17(2004): 1798-1800.

8. Tanielian, "Invisible Wounds."

9. Tanielian, "Invisible Wounds."

10. Blumenshine, "Sacrifices." See also: www.mpls-synod.org/programs/vets

11. Blumenshine, "Sacrifices."

12. Beyond the Yellow Ribbon, www.minnesotanationalguard.org/returning_troops/btyr_overview.php

13. Hoge,"Combat Duty in Iraq."

14. Tanielian, "Invisible Wounds."

15. *In November of 2008 a congressional panel concluded that Gulf War Illnesses (GWI) are "real." For years sufferers were told that their problems were imagined and veterans' questions about toxin exposure were largely dismissed. More than one fourth of the nearly 700,000 veterans who served in Desert Storm, the first Persian Gulf War, suffer from GWI. The primary causes of the illnesses are attributed to two main factors; the drug (Pyridostigmine Bromide) taken in pill form to protect service members against chemical attack and veterans' frequent exposure to the toxic chemicals in pesticides. There is no known cure for many of the conditions caused by exposure to toxins. Sufferers of war-related exposure to toxins and their surviving spouses may not know that they are eligible for benefits. For example, some widows or widowers of Vietnam veterans are still unaware that they are eligible for benefits if their spouse died from complications of illnesses related to Agent Orange exposure, such as diabetes and testicular cancer. The Defense and Veterans Affairs Departments also recognize fibromyalgia, brain cancer, and Lou Gehrig's disease as potentially connected to service during Gulf War I. Because of the high incidence among Gulf War I veterans, Parkinson's disease is being studied as possibly military service related.*

16. Tanielian, "Invisible Wounds."

17. Tanielian, "Invisible Wounds."

18. Hoge,"Combat Duty in Iraq."

19. Coleman, Penny. *Flashback: Posttraumatic Stress Disorder, Suicide, and the Lessons of War.* Boston, MA: Beacon Press, 2007.

20. Tanielian, "Invisible Wounds."

21. Dean, Chuck. *Nam Vet: Making Peace with Your Past.* Kearney, NE: Wordsmith Publishing, 2000: 39.

22. Sadler, Anne, Brenda Booth, and Bradley Doebbeling. "Gang and Multiple Rapes During Military Service: Health Consequences and Health Care." *Journal of the American Medical Women's Association* 60.1 (2005): 33-41.

23. Polusny, Melissa A., and Maureen Murdoch. "Sexual Assault among Male Veterans." Psychiatric Times XXII.4 (2005).
    http://www.psychiatrictimes.com/display/article/10168/52251 (Accessed 30 Aug. 2009)
    See also: Mic Hunter, *Honor Betrayed: Sexual Abuse in America's Military.* Fort Lee, NJ: Barricade Books, 2007.

24. Orban, Michael. *Souled Out: A Memoir of War and Inner Peace.* Candler, North Carolina: Silver Rings Press, 2007:18.

25. Lovollo, William. *Stress and Health: Biological and Psychological Interactions.* Thousand Oaks, CA. Sage Publications, 1997.

26. "Larry's Story." Personal Interview by John Sippola. Used with permission. 1 Nov. 2007.

27. Zemler, John. Personal Interviews by Amy Blumenshine. March 2007.
    See also: www.johnzemler.com. (Accessed 30 Aug. 2009.)

28. Welcome Them Home website, Resources: "How to be a People of Faith in a Time of War."
    www.welcomethemhomebook.com (Accessed 15 Sept. 2009.)

About the Authors

Amy Blumenshine, MSW, MART (Religion and Theology), is a candidate for the diaconal ministry in the ELCA. Ministry with veterans and their families is her specialty. In July of 2005, she convened the Coming Home Collaborative to engage faith communities and health professionals in reducing the secondary trauma veterans and their families often experience. The Coming Home Collaborative, based at Our Saviour's Lutheran Church, Minneapolis, with support from its neighbor, Walk-In Counseling Center, is an open and growing volunteer association of people who are concerned with the psychological and spiritual healing of veterans, especially those currently re-integrating with their families and communities. Amy taught crisis intervention for a decade at Metropolitan State University in St. Paul, Minnesota, and has served in a number of crisis intervention settings. She has published on this topic in the *Inter-Lutheran Journal of Pastoral Care* (Caring Connections Online). She and her family also served for two years as ELCA lay missionaries in Nicaragua. Amy's father was a veteran. The Coming Home Collaborative materials are published on the Minneapolis Synod website **www.mpls-synod.org.**

John Sippola, MDiv, has served as a parish pastor for 20 years and as a hospital chaplain for 15 years. A chaplain (ret.) in the Minnesota Army National Guard, John served as the Family Assistance Center chaplain in Duluth, Minnesota during the first Persian Gulf War. During that time, he helped facilitate support groups for spouses and parents, and co-led a support group for the children of deployed service members. As a hospital chaplain, he worked extensively with veterans in chemical dependency and mental health settings. From 1997–2000, John served as the Family Assistance Chaplain for the State of Minnesota. John is convinced that churches have a strategic role in promoting relational and spiritual well-being of returning veterans and their families. John is privileged to be pastor of Elim Lutheran Church of Blackhoof in Barnum, Minnesota, a co-sponsor of this project.

Donald A Tubesing, PhD, MDiv, is a retired ELCA pastor. He holds a PhD in Counselor Education from Ohio University and a Master of Divinity degree from Concordia Seminary, St Louis. In 1973, with a grant from the Kellogg Foundation, he helped the church-based Wholistic Health Centers Project develop as well as the National Parish Nurse Program. In 1977 he founded Whole Person Associates, a training and publishing company focused on providing stress management and wellness promotion educational materials for professionals in medicine, ministry, social work and counseling. Over the past 30 years, he has trained over 10,000 professionals in the skills of designing and conducting stress and wellness workshops with a whole person focus and has served as consultant to several military health programs. Don is author of 21 books on stress management and wellness promotion. He has also served as president of the 4,000 member Independent Book Publishers Association. Don grew up on the grounds of several VA Hospitals—his father having served his career as a chaplain. Don dedicates his efforts on this project to the honor of his father's life-long commitment to the ongoing care of veterans.

Valerie Yancey, PhD, is an Associate Professor of Nursing at Southern Illinois University, Edwardsville. She holds certifications in Holistic Nursing, Hospice and Palliative Care Nursing, and Stress Management. Dr. Yancey teaches courses in holistic care and the spiritual dimensions of health and healing. As a bedside critical-care nurse for 25 years, she learned the importance of caring for the whole person—body, mind and spirit—and teaches others about the healing potential of spiritual care. She has educated baccalaureate and graduate level nurses for 30 years and provides educational experiences for parish nurses in congregational ministries. Theologically, Valerie understands how veterans give us all insight into our collective need for God's Promise, as we journey together through trauma into health, healing, and hope.